IT DEPENDS

IT DEPENDS

Writing on Technology Leadership 2012-2022

KEVIN GOLDSMITH

Unit Circle Press

for Nicole and Oakley

CONTENTS

AGILE — 183

LEADING ORGANIZATIONS — 197

Introduction

Like many technology leaders, I started my career as a software developer. I was excited about new technologies and the process of building and innovating in code. My first "management" roles came as I was still figuring out who I was as a developer. Suddenly, I was thrust into being responsible for an intern or an entire team of developers more experienced than myself without any training or support. Sadly, this path to management was very common in the 1990s in the software industry. It is still all too common, unfortunately.

As my professional maturity increased, I continued to bounce between individual and management roles. I didn't have a plan for my career. My role would be dictated more by the needs of my manager or the company than my preference.

I joined Adobe in 2004 as a developer on a brand new team working on innovative technologies for the Creative Suite. I had a great manager, John Metzger. Adobe was the first company I worked at where the role of a manager was distinct from that of a developer or tech lead. I began to understand more about the job of the manager there.

My team was reorganized in 2005 to be the developers for a new framework that the Adobe Research team was creating, the Adobe Image Foundation, advanced technology for heterogenous image and video processing using GPUs, and the latest multi-core CPU architectures. The team manager was the head of Adobe Research, Gavin Miller, but as the goal was to productize the work, he would not lead the team long-term.

With my new understanding of management, I interviewed and was hired to become the team's manager. I threw myself into learning as much about my new role as I had in learning how to be a better developer. Sadly, there weren't many resources for an aspiring technology leader in the mid-2000s. I took every class that Adobe offered (a great resource, but very generic to "management") and read every book I could find (much of the "management" literature then was still in the vein of old-school large-company management practices, including recommendations for Sun Tsu's The Art of War).

Inspired by Michael Lopp's Rands in Repose[1] blog, I decided to share what I learned from others and my experience growing as a manager. My blog, Puppies, Flowers, Rainbows, and Kittens[2], was not originally a technology or management blog. The name demonstrates that, as does my tagline, "Sarcasm and vitriol wrapped in a twee bow." I was not aiming to be an influencer, just to share what I learned. I will also be the first to admit that I am not a dedicated blogger or a particularly good writer. My posts were infrequent and would have benefited from a critical editorial eye. I persisted, though, buoyed by the occasional encounter with someone who had read a post and found value in it. The quality of my writing improved with practice, although my posting frequency did not.

Over the years, as I created my infrequent posts, others seeing the same absence of resources for developing or aspiring technology leaders also worked to address the gap. Now a new technology manager has shelves of books and multiple conferences and courses they can attend. This abundance of learning material is exciting, and I enjoy learning from my peers. I continue to share, but now I can focus on sharing the unique lessons I have learned after more than 30 years in the industry with the perspective that has brought me.

In 2020, as the world found new hobbies as we all locked down for COVID-19, I started reflecting on the body of writing I had amassed over the years. Rereading old posts, I found bits of wisdom that I think are still valuable.

I also started to sense a theme with my writing and something that I didn't see in the writing of others, which is how the unique context of the situation you are in must guide your decisions. I would recommend a book to someone I mentor, but nearly always with the caveat that "you should understand that the author has only worked in these kinds of companies, and so you should take their prescriptive advice with a pinch of salt."

Sometimes, when someone asked if I would ever write a book of my own, I would say that if I did, the title would be "It Depends" because so often, I would caveat an answer to a question with the circumstance that framed that answer.

So, during my quarantine with my family, I started collecting my old blog posts, reformatting them, and editing them with my improved writing expertise and the never-tiring but occasionally tiresome help of Grammarly. While I intended to improve readability, I did not want to alter the original message of each article.

You will see a few messages from recent me, clearly marked, where I want to correct or amend my younger self, but I left the original content in place. Each article is still available on my blog, which remains intact if you feel like comparing.

I hope you find this book helpful in your journey to becoming a more thoughtful technology leader.

Kevin Goldsmith, August 2023

Engineering Culture

Your company's engineering culture determines how the work is done, how much control you have over the work in your team, what behaviors will get you promoted, and which will get you fired.

There is no perfect engineering culture, my experience at Microsoft in the 1990s was diametrically the opposite of my experience at Spotify twenty years later, but both companies were dominant in their parts of the technology industry.

It is more important to support a culture for your team that is in harmony with your larger company culture than to try to adopt another company's culture. Learn from everyone, but build something bespoke for your team.

CHAPTER 1

Fail Safe, Fail Smart... Succeed!

Originally published on December 30, 2020

THE IMPORTANCE OF FAILURE IN SOFTWARE DEVELOPMENT

How we approach failure is critical in any industry, but it is especially crucial in building software.

Why?

The answer is simple: **invention requires failure.**

We don't acknowledge that fact enough as an industry. Not broadly. It is something we should recognize and understand more. Technologists continually look for ways to transform existing businesses or build new products. We are an industry that grows on innovation and invention.

Real innovation is creating something uniquely new. If you can create something genuinely novel without failing a few times along the way, it probably isn't very innovative. As Albert Einstein said:

> "Anyone who has never made a mistake has never tried anything new."
>
> ALBERT EINSTEIN

In his own words, Thomas Edison said that he created three thousand theories before finding suitable materials for his electric light.

Filmmaker Kevin Smith says, "Failure is success training." I like that sentiment. It frames failure as leading to success.

Failure teaches you the things you need to know to succeed. Stated more strongly: **failure is a requirement for success.**

CREATING A FAIL-SAFE ENVIRONMENT

To achieve success, what's important isn't avoiding failure; it is handling failure when it comes. The handling of failure makes the difference between eventual success and never succeeding. Creating conditions conducive to learning from failure means creating a fail-safe environment.

In the software industry, we used to define a fail-safe environment as an environment with many processes to avoid failure. Instead, we should ensure that when the inevitable failure happens, we handle it well and reduce its impact. We want to **fail smart.**

When I was at Spotify, a company that worked hard to create a fail-smart environment, we described this as "minimizing the blast radius." This quote from Mikael Krantz, the head architect at Spotify during that time, sums up the idea nicely:

> "We want to be an internal combustion engine, not a fuel-air bomb. Many small, controlled explosions, propelling us in a generally ok direction, not a huge blast leveling half the city."
>
> **MIKAEL KRANTZ**

So, let us plan for failure. Let's embrace the mistakes that will come in the most thoughtful way possible. Then, we can use those failures to move us forward and ensure they are small enough not to take out the company. I like the combustion engine analogy because it embraces that a well-handled failure still pushes us in the right direction. If we anticipate, we can course-correct and continue to move forward.

One way to create these small, controlled explosions is to **fail fast**. Find the fastest, most straightforward path to learning. Can you validate your idea quickly? Can you reduce the scope so that you can get it in front of real people immediately and get feedback before investing in a bunch of work?

A side benefit of small failures is that they are easier to understand. You can identify what happened and learn from it. With a big failure, you must unpack and dig in to know where things went wrong.

THE LESSON OF CLIPPY

Figure 1 - Clippy
Microsoft Corporation

Even if you've never used the Office Assistant feature of Microsoft Office[3], you are likely aware of it. It was a software product flop so massive that it became a part of pop culture[4].

I worked at Microsoft when the company created Office Assistant. Although I didn't work on that team, I knew a few people who did.

It is easy to think that the Office Assistant was a horrible idea created by a group of poor-performing developers and product people, but that couldn't be farther from the truth. Clippy was built by highly talented developers, product leads, researchers with fantastic track records, and PhDs from top-tier universities. People who thought they understood the market and their users. These world-class people were working on one of (if not THE) most successful software products of all time at the apex of its popularity. Microsoft spent millions of dollars and many person-years on the development of Clippy.

So, what happened?

What happened is that those brilliant people were wrong. Very wrong, as all of us are from time to time. How could they have found their mistake before releasing widely? It wasn't easy at the time to test product assumptions. It was much harder to validate hypotheses about users and their needs then compared to today.

How we used to release software

Before we could assume high-bandwidth internet connections, we wrote and shipped software in a very different way.

Software products were manufactured, transcribed onto plastic and foil discs. For a release like Microsoft Office, those discs were manufactured in countries worldwide, put into boxes, then put onto trucks and trains and shipped to warehouses, like TV sets. From there, trucks would take them to stores where people would purchase them in person, take them home and spend an afternoon swapping the discs in and out of their computers, installing the software.

With a release like Office, Microsoft would need massive disc pressing capability. It required dozens of CD/DVD plants across the world to work simultaneously. That capability had to be booked years in advance. Microsoft would pay massive sums to take over the capacity of the entire CD/DVD pressing industry. This monopolization of disc manufacturing required a fixed duration. Moving or growing that window was monstrously expensive.

It was challenging to validate a new feature in that atmosphere, particularly if it was a significant part of a release that you didn't want to leak to the press.

That was then; this is now

Today, the world is very different. There is no excuse for not validating your ideas.

You can now deploy your website every time you hit save in your editor. You can ship your mobile app multiple times per week. You can try ideas almost as fast as you can think of them. You can try and fail, learn from the failure, and improve your product continuously.

> "If you want to increase your success rate, double your failure rate."
>
> THOMAS J. WATSON
> *CEO OF IBM FROM 1914-1956*

If it takes you years and millions of dollars to fail, and you want to double that, your company will not survive to see eventual success. **Failing Fast minimizes the impact of your failure by reducing the cost and delay in learning.**

I worked at an IBM research lab a long time ago. I was a developer on a project building early versions of synchronized streaming media. After over a year of effort, we arranged to publish our work. As we prepared, we learned that two other IBM labs were working on the same problems. Our work was complete; it was too late to collaborate. At the time, it seemed to me like big-company stupidity, not realizing that three different teams were working on the same thing. Later, I realized that this was a deliberate choice. It was how IBM failed fast. Since it took too long to fail serially, IBM had become good at failing in parallel.

BUILDING A FAIL-SAFE CULTURE

If innovation requires failure to build an innovative product or company, how your culture handles the inevitable failures is key to creating a fail-safe environment.

Many companies still punish projects or features that do not succeed. The same companies then wonder why their employees are so risk-averse. Punishing failure can take many forms, both obvious and subtle. For example, punishment can mean firing the team or leader who created an unsuccessful release or project.

Sanctions can be more subtle:

- Moving resources away from innovative efforts that don't yield immediate successes.
- Allowing people to ridicule failed efforts.
- Continuing to invest in the slow, steady growth projects instead of the more innovative but risky efforts. The innovator's dilemma[5] is just the most well-known aspect of this.

Breeding innovation out

I spent several years working at a company whose leadership constantly encouraged employees to be more innovative and take more risks. It created ever-new incentives to incite new products from the organization. It was also a company that had consistently grown through acquisition. Every year, it would acquire new companies. At the start of the following year's budget process, there would inevitably be the realization that the company had grown too large. Nearly every year, there would be a layoff.

Where would you look if you are a senior leader and need to trim ten percent of your organization? In previous years, you likely had already eliminated your lowest performers. Should you reduce the funding of the products that bring in your revenue or kill the new products struggling to make their first profit? The answer is clear if your bonus and salary depend on hitting revenue targets.

No matter what the intentions of the company were, through its actions, it communicated that taking risks was detrimental to a career. So, the company lost its most entrepreneurial employees through voluntary or involuntary attrition. Because it could not innovate within, innovation could only happen through acquisitions, perpetuating the cycle.

If you overtly or subtly punish failure, and failure is necessary for innovation, then you are disincentivizing innovation.

Don't punish failure. Punish not learning from failure. Punish failing big when you could have failed small first. Better yet, don't punish at all. Instead, reward the failures that produce essential lessons for the company that the team handles well. Reward risk-taking if you want to encourage innovation.

If you worry about employees taking risks without accountability, give them participation in the revenue that they bring in (see the chapter "The Myth of a Startup in a Large Company").

EACH FAILURE ALLOWS YOU TO LEARN MANY THINGS. TAKE THE TIME TO LEARN THOSE LESSONS

Learning from failure

It can be hard to learn the lessons from failure. When you fail, your instinct is to move on, to sweep it under the rug. You don't want to wallow in your mistakes. However, if you move on too quickly, you miss the chance to gather all the lessons, leading to more failure instead of the success you seek.

Lessons from failure: Your process

Sometimes the failure was in your process. The following exchange is fictional, but I've heard something very much like it more than once in my career.

> *"What happened with this release? Customers are complaining that it is incredibly buggy."*

> *"Well, the test team was working on a different project, so they jumped into this one late. We didn't want to delay the release, so we cut the time for testing short and didn't catch those issues. We had test automation, and it caught some of the issues, but*

there have been a lot of false positives, so no one was watching the results."

"Did we do a beta test for this release? An employee release?"

"No."

The above conversation indicates a problem with the software development process (and, for this specific example, a culture-of-quality problem). If you've ever had an exchange like the one above, what did you do to solve the underlying issues? If the answer is "not much," you didn't learn enough from the failure, and you likely continued to have similar problems afterward.

Lessons from failure: your team

Sometimes, your team is a significant factor in a failure. I don't mean the group members aren't good at their jobs. Your team may be missing a skillset or have personality conflicts. Trust may be an issue within the team, so people aren't open with each other.

"The app is performing incredibly slowly. What is going on?"

"Well, we inherited this component that uses this data store, and no one on the team understands it. So, we're learning as we do it, and it has become a performance problem."

Suppose the above exchange happened in your team. In that case, you might make sure that the next time you decide to use (or inherit) a technology, you make sure that someone on the team knows it well, even if that means adding someone to the team.

Lessons from failure: your perception of your customers

A vein of failure, and a significant one in the lessons of Clippy, is having an incorrect mental model for your customer.

We all have myths about who our customers are. Why do I call them "myths"? The reason is that you can't precisely read the minds of every one of your customers. At the beginning of a product's life cycle, when there are few customers, you may know each of them well. That condition, hopefully, will not last very long.

How do you build a model of your user? First, you do user research, talk to your customer service team, beta test, and read app reviews and tweets about your product. Next, you read your product forums. Finally, you instrument your app and analyze user behavior.

We have many ways of interacting with subsets of our customers. Those interactions give us the feeling that we know what they want or who they are.

These exchanges provide insights into your customers as an aggregate. They also fuel myths about who our customers are because they are a sampling of the whole. We can't know all our customers, so we create personas in our minds or collectively for our team.

Suppose you have a great user research team and are rigorous in your efforts to understand your customers. You may be able to have in-depth knowledge about your users and their needs for your product. However, that knowledge and understanding will be transitory. Your product continues to evolve and change and hopefully add new users often. Your new customers come to your product because of the unique problems they can solve using it. Those problems differ from existing users—your perception of your customers ages quickly. You are now building for who they were, not who they are.

Lessons from failure: your understanding of your product

You may think you understand your product; after all, you are the one who is building it! However, *the product your customers are using may differ from the product you are making.*

You build your product to solve a problem. In your effort to solve that problem, you may also solve other problems for your customers that you didn't anticipate. Your customers are delighted that they can solve this problem with your product. In their minds, this was a deliberate choice on your part.

Now you make a change that improves the original problem's solution but breaks the unintended use case. Your customers are angry because you ruined their product!

Lessons from failure: yourself

Failure gives you a chance to learn more about yourself. Is there something you could do differently next time? Did an external factor become obvious in hindsight that could have been detected earlier if you had approached things differently?

Our failures tend to be the hardest to dwell on. Our natural inclination is to find fault externally to console ourselves. Instead, it is worth taking some time to reflect on your performance. You will always find something you can do that will help you the next time.

COLLECTING THE LESSONS: PROJECT RETROSPECTIVES

The best way that I have learned to extract the lessons is to do a project retrospective.

A project retrospective aims to understand what happened in the project from its inception to its conclusion. You want to understand each critical decision, what informed the decision, and its outcome.

In a project retrospective, you are looking for the things that went wrong, the things that went well, and the things that went well but you could do better the next time. The output of the retrospective is neutral. It is not for establishing blame or awarding kudos. Instead, it exists to make sure your team learns. For this reason, it is helpful for both unsuccessful and highly successful projects.

A good practice for creating a great culture around failure is to make it the general custom to have a retrospective at the end of every project in your company. Having retrospectives only for unsuccessful projects perpetuates a blame culture.

THE PROJECT RETROSPECTIVE REPOSITORY

Since the project retrospectives are blameless, it is good to share them within your company. Create a project retrospective repository and publicize it.

The repository becomes a precious resource for everyone in your company. It shows what has worked and what has been challenging in your environment. It allows your teams to avoid making the mistakes of the past. We always want to be making new mistakes, not old ones!

The repository is also handy for new employees to teach them how projects work in your company. Finally, it is also a resource for documenting product decisions.

The retrospective repository is a valuable place to capture your products' history and process.

SPOTIFY'S FAILURE-SAFE CULTURE

I learned a lot about creating a failure-safe culture while working at Spotify. Some of the great examples of this culture were:

**Figure 2 - A "fail wall" whiteboard with
sticky notes of lessons**

One of the squads created a "Fail Wall" to capture the things they were learning. The squad didn't hide the wall. Instead, it was on a whiteboard facing the hallway where everyone could see it.

**Figure 3 - Google Document of a project
retrospective**

This document is a report from one of the project retrospectives. You don't need any special software for the record. For us, it was just a collection of Google docs in a shared folder.

#fail-wall
This is the very beginning of the #fail-wall channel, which was created by cessan today. Purpose: The purpose of this channel is to celebrate failure! Share your failures no matter how big or small they are. Learn from others failure. Direct people here who are afraid of failing. (edit)

Figure 4 - "Fail wall" Slack channel

One of the agile coaches created a Slack channel for teams to share the lessons learned from failures with the whole company.

Figure 5 - "Celebrate Failures" blog post

Spotify's CTO posted an article encouraging everyone to celebrate the lessons they learned from failure. Which inspired other posts like this:

Figure 6 - Spotify Engineering blog post

If you look at the Spotify engineering blog[6], there are probably more posts about mistakes than cool things we did in the years I worked there (2013-2016).

These kinds of posts are also valuable to the community. When you are searching for something, it is because you are having a problem. We might have had the same issue. These posts are also very public expressions of the company culture.

FAILURE AS A COMPETITIVE ADVANTAGE

We're all going to fail as we attempt to innovate. If my company can fail smart and fast, learning from our mistakes, while your company ignores the lessons from failure, my company will have a competitive advantage.

MAKING FAILURE SAFER

How do we reduce the fuel-air bomb failure into an internal combustion failure? How can we fail safely?

Minimizing the cost of failure

Figure 7 - "Think it, Build it, Ship it,
Tweak it" sign at Spotify's Headquarters
in Stockholm.

If you fail quickly, you are reducing the cost in time, equipment, and expenses. At Spotify, we used a framework rooted in Lean Startup[7] to reduce the cost of our failures. We named the framework "Think it, Build it, Ship it, Tweak it."[8]

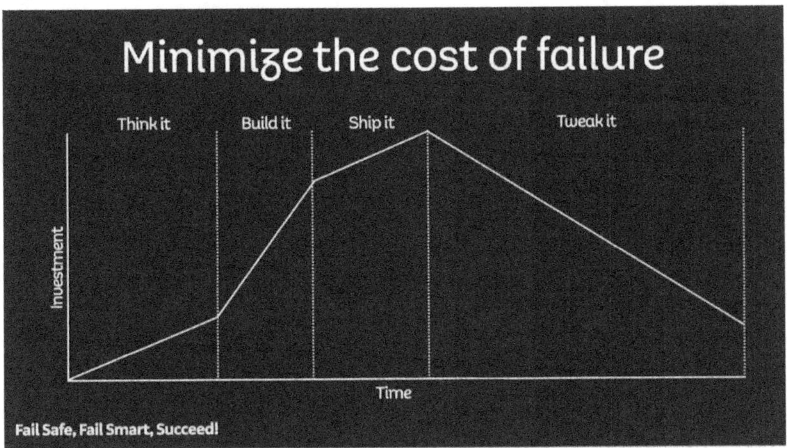

Figure 8 - Chart showing the cost of a feature or product development over time

This graph shows investment into a feature over time through the different phases of the framework. Investment here signifies people's time, material costs, equipment, opportunity cost, whichever.

Think It

Imagine this scenario: you are a developer returning from lunch with some people you work with, and you have an idea for a new feature. You discuss it with your product owner, and they like the idea. So, you decide to explore if it would be a valuable feature for the product. You have now entered the "Think It" phase. During this phase, you may work with the Product Owner and potentially a designer. This phase represents a part-time effort by a small subset of the team—a small investment.

You might create paper prototypes to test the idea with the team and customers. You may develop some lightweight code prototypes. You may even ship a very early version of the feature to some users. The goal is to test as quickly and cheaply as possible and gather objective data on the feature's viability.

You build a hypothesis on how the feature can positively impact the product, tied to real product metrics. This hypothesis is what you will validate against at each stage of the framework.

If the early data shows that customers don't need or want the feature, your hypothesis is incorrect. You have two choices. You may iterate and try a different permutation of the concept, staying in the Think It phase and keeping the investment low. You may decide it wasn't as good an idea as you hoped and end the effort before investing further.

If you decide to end during the Think It phase, congratulations! You've saved the company time and money building something unnecessary. Collect the lessons in a retrospective and share them so everyone else can learn.

Build It

The initial tests look promising. The hypothesis isn't validated, but the indicators warrant further investment. You have some direction from your tests for the first version of the feature.

Now is the time to build the feature for real. The investment increases substantially as the rest of the team gets involved.

How can you reduce the cost of failure in the Build It phase? First, you don't build the fully realized conception of the feature. Instead, you develop the smallest version that will validate your initial hypothesis, the MVP (Minimum Viable Product)[9]. Your goal is validation with the broader customer set.

The Build It phase is where many companies I speak to get stuck. If you have the complete product vision in your head, finding a minimal representation seems like a weak concept. Folks in love with their ideas have difficulty finding the core element that validates the whole. Suppose the initial data that comes back for the MVP puts the hypothesis into question. In that case, it is easier to question the validity of the MVP than to examine the hypothesis's validity. This issue of MVP is usually the most significant source of contention in the process.

It takes practice to figure out how to formulate a good MVP, but the effort is worth it. Imagine if the Clippy team had been able to ship an MVP. Better early feedback could have saved many person-years and millions of dollars. In my career, I have spent years (literally) building a product without shipping it. Our team's leadership shifted product directions several times without validating or invalidating any of their hypotheses in the market. We learned nothing about the product opportunity, but the development team learned much about refactoring and building modular code.

Even during the Build It phase, there are opportunities to test the hypothesis: early internal releases, beta tests, user tests, and limited A/B tests can all be used to provide direction and information.

Ship It

Your MVP is ready to release to your customers! The validation with the limited release pools and the user testing shows that your hypothesis may be valid–time to ship.

In many companies, if not most, shipping a software release is still a binary thing. No users have it, and now all users have it. This approach robs you of an opportunity to fail cheaply! Your testing in Think It and Build It may have validated your hypothesis. However, it may have also provided incorrect information, or you may have misinterpreted it. On the technical side, whatever you have done to this point will not validate that your software performs correctly at scale.

Instead of shipping instantly to one hundred percent of your users, do a progressive rollout[10]. At Spotify, we had the benefit of a massive scale. This scale allowed us to ship to 1%, 5%, 10%, 25%, 50%, and then 99% of our users (we usually held back 1% of our users as a control group for some time). Due to our size, we could do this rollout relatively quickly while maintaining statistical significance[11].

If you have a smaller user base, you can still do this with fewer steps and get much of the value.

At each rollout stage, we'd use product analytics to see if we were validating our assumptions. Remember that we always tied the hypothesis back to product metrics. We'd also watch our systems to ensure they were handling the load appropriately and had no other technical issues or bugs arising.

If the analytics showed that we weren't improving the product, we had two decisions again. Should we iterate and try different permutations of the idea, or should we stop and remove the feature?

Usually, if we reached this point, we would iterate, keeping to the same percentage of users. If this feature MVP wasn't adding to the product, it took away from it, so rolling out further would be a bad idea. This rollout process was another way to reduce the cost of failure. It reduced the percentage of users seeing a change that may negatively affect product metrics. Sometimes, iterating and testing with a subset of users would give us the necessary information to move forward with a better version of the MVP. Occasionally, we would realize that the hypothesis was invalid. We would then remove the feature (which is just as hard to do as you imagine, but it was more comfortable with data validating the decision).

If we had removed the feature during the Ship It phase, we would have wasted time and money. However, we still would have squandered less than if we'd released a lousy feature to our entire customer base.

Tweak It

You have now released the MVP for the feature to all your customers. The product metrics validate the hypothesis that it is improving the product. You are now ready for the next and final phase, Tweak It.

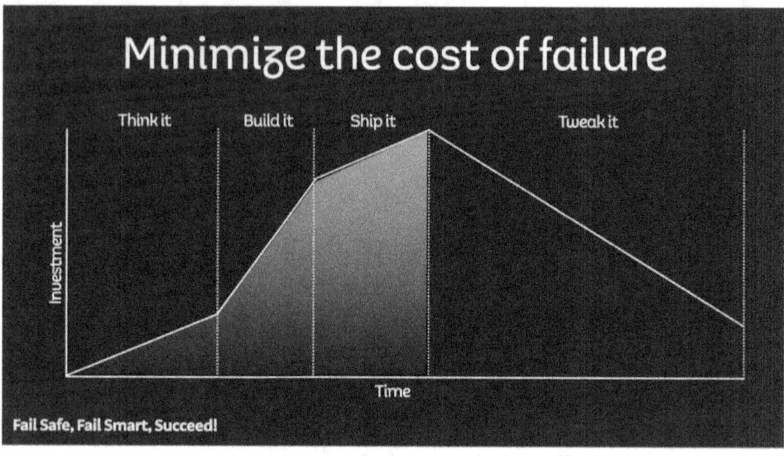

Figure 9 - Think It/Build It/Ship It/Tweak It

The shaded area under this graph shows the investment to get a feature to customers. Until you release the feature to all your customers, you will not earn anything against the investment. Until that point, you are just spending resources. The Think It/ Ship It/Build It/Tweak It framework aims to reduce that shaded area and the investment amount before you start seeing a return.

The MVP does not realize the full product vision, and the metrics may be positive but not to the level of your hypothesis. There is a lot more opportunity here!

The result of the Ship It phase represents a new baseline for the product and the feature. The real-world usage data, customer support, reviews, forums, and user research can now inform your next steps.

The Tweak It phase represents a series of smaller Think It/ Build It/Ship It/Tweak It efforts. From now, your team iteratively improves the shipped version of the feature and establishes new, better baselines. These efforts will involve less and less of the team over time, and the investment will decrease correspondingly.

When iterating, occasionally, you reach a local maximum. Your tweaks will result in smaller and smaller improvements to the product. Once again, you have two choices: move on to the next feature or look for another substantial opportunity with the current feature.

The difficulty is recognizing that there may be a much bigger opportunity nearby. When you reach this decision point, it can be beneficial to try a big experiment. On the other hand, you may also take a step back and look for an opportunity that might be orthogonal to the original vision but could provide a significant improvement.

You notice in the graph that the investment never reaches zero. This gap reveals the secret, hidden fifth step of the framework.

Maintain It

Even if there is no active development on a feature, it doesn't mean there isn't any investment. The feature takes up space in the product, hogging valuable UI real estate and making it harder to add other new features. The code may be prone to breaking with library or system updates and will be the source of user-reported bugs. Maintaining documentation as the product evolves is also a burden.

The investment cost means it is critical not to add features to a product that do not demonstrably improve it. There is no such thing as a zero-cost feature. Suppose new functionality adds nothing to the product in terms of incremental value to users.

In that case, the company must still invest in maintaining it. Features that bring slight improvements to core metrics may not be worth preserving, given the additional complexity they add.

EXPECT FAILURE ALL THE TIME

There is a substantial difference in how we discuss failure in the context of software development from the year 2000 compared to today. Back then, you worked hard to write robust software, but there was an expectation of hardware reliability. So, when a hardware failure occurred, the software's fault tolerance was of incidental importance. Of course, you didn't want to cause errors yourself, but if the platform was unstable, there wasn't much you were expected to do about it.

Today we live in a world with public clouds and mobile platforms where the environment is entirely beyond our control. Amazon's Web Services platform taught us a lot about handling system failure. A blog post from Netflix about their move to AWS[12] was pivotal to the industry's adapting to the new world. The blog post discusses how Netflix had to change their perception of how services work because Infrastructure as a Service platforms like AWS work very differently to traditional corporate data centers.

Netflix's approach to system design has been so beneficial to the industry. We now assume that everything can be on fire all the time. You could write perfect software, and the scheduler will still come and kill it on mobile. AWS will kill your process, and your service will be moved from one pod to another without warning. We now write our software expecting failure to happen at any time.

We've learned that writing large systems complicates handling failure, and one of the reasons micro-service architectures have become more prevalent is to help us be failure safe. Why? Because they are significantly more fault-tolerant, they fail small when they fail. Products like Amazon, Netflix, and Spotify all have large numbers of services running. A customer doesn't notice if one or more instances of the services fail. When a service fails in those environments, it is responsible for a small part of the experience. The other systems assume it can fail. There are things like caching to compensate for a system disappearing.

Netflix has its famous chaos monkey[13] testing, which randomly kills services or even entire availability zones in their production environment. These tests make sure that their systems fail well.

An architecture composed of smaller services that are assumed to fail means that there is near zero user impact when there is a problem. Therefore, failing well is critical for these services and their user experience.

Smaller services also make it possible to use DevOps techniques such as progressive rollout,[14] feature flags,[15] dark launching,[16] blue-green deploys,[17] and canary instances,[18] making it easier to build in a fail-safe way.

MY BIGGEST FAILURE

If you are a long-time Spotify user, you probably won't recognize the interface shown in the photo below. In May of

2015, though, Spotify was very interested in telling the whole world about it. It was a new set of features in the product called "Spotify Now[19]."

Figure 10 - Spotify Now

I led the engineering effort at Spotify on the Spotify Now set of features. It was the most extensive concerted effort that Spotify had done to that time, involving hundreds of employees worldwide.

Spotify Now was a set of features built around bringing the perfect, personalized music for every user for every moment of the day. This effort included adding video, podcasts, a Running feature, a massive collection of new editorial and machine learning-generated playlists, and a simplified user interface for accessing music. It was audacious for a reason. We knew that Apple would launch its Apple Music streaming product soon. So, we wanted to make a public statement that we were the most innovative platform. Our goal was to take the wind out of Apple's sails (and sales!)

Given that this was Spotify, we understood how to fail smart.

As we launched the project, I reviewed the project retrospective repository. I wanted to see what had and had not worked on large projects before. With that knowledge, I was now prepared to make all new mistakes instead of repeating ones from the past.

We had a tight timeline, but some features were already in development. I felt confident. However, there was a growing concern as we moved forward, and the new features started to take shape in the employee releases. We worried the new features wouldn't be as compelling as the vision we had for them. We knew that we, as employees, were not the target users of Spotify Now. We were not representative of our users. To truly understand how the functionality would perform, we wanted to follow our usual product development methods and get the features in front of real customers to validate our hypotheses.

Publicly releasing the features to a narrow audience was a challenge at that time. The press, aware of Apple's impending launch, closely watched every Spotify release. They knew that we tested features and were looking for hints of what we would do to counter Apple.

Our marketing team wanted a big launch event. This release was a statement. We wanted a massive spike in Spotify's press coverage, extolling our innovation. The response would be muted if Spotify Now leaked before the event.

There was pressure from Marketing not to test the features, but Product Engineering wanted to follow our standard validation processes. Eventually, we found a compromise. We released early versions of Spotify Now to a relatively small cohort of New Zealand users. Then, satisfied that we were now testing the features in the market, we went back to building and preparing for the launch while waiting for the test results.

After a few weeks, we got fantastic news. Our cohort's retention was 6% higher than the rest of our customer base.

Customer retention is the most critical metric for a subscription-based product like Spotify. It determines the Lifetime Value[20] of the customer. The longer you use a subscription product, the more money the company will make.

With a company of the scale of Spotify, it was tough to significantly move a core metric like retention. A whole point percentage move was rare and something to celebrate. With Spotify Now, we had a 6% increase! It was a massive result.

Now, all our doubt was gone. We knew we were working on something exceptional. Finally, we'd validated it in the market! With real people!

On the launch day, Daniel Ek, Spotify's CEO and founder; Gustav Söderstrom, the Chief Product Officer; and Rochelle King, the head of Spotify's design organization, shared a stage in New York with famous musicians and television personalities. They walked through everything we had built. It was a lovely event. Simultaneously, I shared a stage in the company's headquarters in Stockholm with Shiva Rajaraman and Dan Sormaz, my product and design peers. We watched the event with our team, celebrating.

As soon as the event concluded, we started the rollout of the new features by releasing them to 1% of our customers in our four most significant markets. We'd begun our Ship It phase! We drank champagne and ate prinsesstårta (my favorite Swedish cake).

I couldn't wait to see how the features were doing in the market. After so much work, I wanted to start the progressive rollout to 100%. Daily, I would stop by the desk of the data analyst who monitored the metrics. He sent me away for the first couple of days with the comment, "it is too early still. We're not even close to statistical significance." Then one day, instead, he said, "It is still too early to be sure, but we're starting to see the trend take shape, and it doesn't look like it will be as high as we'd hoped." Every day after, his expression became dourer. Finally, it was official. Instead of the 6% increase we'd seen in testing, the new features produced a 1% decrease in retention. It was a 7% difference between what we had tested and what we had launched.

Not only were our new features not enticing customers to stay longer on our platform, we were driving them away! To say that this was a problem was an understatement. It was a colossal failure.

Now we had an enormous quandary. We had failed big instead of small. We had released several things together, so finding the problem was challenging. Additionally, we'd just had a major press event where we talked about all these features. There was coverage all over the internet. The world was now waiting for access to what we had promised, but we would lose customers if we rolled them out further.

Those results began one of the most challenging summers of our lives. First, we had to narrow down what was killing our retention in these new features. Then, we had to start generating new hypotheses and running tests within our cohort to find out what had gone wrong.

The challenge was that the cohort was too small to run tests quickly (and it was shrinking daily as we lost customers).

Eventually, we had to do the math to determine how much money the company would lose if we expanded the cohort so our tests would run faster. The cost was determined to be justified, so we grew the testing cohort to 5% of the users in our top four markets.

Gradually, we figured out what in Spotify Now was causing users to quit the product. So, we removed those features and were able to roll out the remainder of the capabilities to the rest of the world with a more modest retention gain.

In the many retrospectives that followed to understand what mistakes we'd made (and what we had done correctly), we found failures in our perceptions of our customers, our teams, and other areas.

It turns out that one of our biggest problems was a process failure. We had a bug in our A/B testing framework. That bug meant that we had accidentally rolled out our Spotify Now test to a cohort participating in a very different trial. A trial to establish a floor on what having no advertising in the free product would do for retention, essentially giving our premium product away for free.

To Spotify's immense credit, instead of punishing me, my peers, and the team, we were rewarded for how we handled the failure. The lessons we learned from the mistakes of Spotify Now were immensely beneficial to the company. Moreover, those lessons produced some of the company's triumphs in the years that have followed, including Spotify's most popular curated playlists, Discover Weekly, Release Radar, Daily Mixes, and podcasts.

PUTTING THIS INTO PRACTICE AT AVVO

If you think you would like to use these ideas at your company but are unsure where to start, I will describe what we did at Avvo. I joined the company as CTO after I left Spotify. When I joined, the company was already nine years old. It had a primarily monolithic architecture running in a single data center with minimal redundancy.

We did some things quickly to move to a more fail-safe world.

Moving from planning around objectives to planning around priorities

First, we worked to build a supportive culture that could handle the inevitable failures better. We moved from planning around specific deliverable commitments to organizing our work around priorities.

Suppose my specific achievements, my output, measure my performance. This way of measuring performance often creates problems.

Suppose I need to coordinate with another person, and their commitments do not align with mine. That situation will create tension. If the company's needs change, but my obligations do not, there is little incentive for me to reorient my work. Dependencies can thwart me from achieving my commitments, or I may need to hamper the company's priorities to achieve my own if they are not well-aligned.

People in leadership like quarterly goals or Management By Objectives[21] because they create strict accountability. If I commit to doing something and it is not complete when I say it will be, I have failed even if it is no longer the right thing for me to do.

Suppose you think instead about aligning around priorities. In that case, those priorities may change from time to time. Still, if everyone is working against the same set of priorities, you can be sure that they are broadly doing the right things for the company. **Aligning to priorities sets an expectation of outcome, not output.**

Talk about failure with an eye to future improvement instead of blame

The senior leadership team must be in alignment with these approaches. The rest of the organization may not be initially. Leaders must communicate with a learning message rather than blame or punishment when discussing failure. People should know that the expectation is that they may fail. If they primarily try to avoid failure, they probably aren't thinking big enough. It is the message: "we want to see you fail, small, and we want to make sure we learn from that failure."

I created our "Fail Wall" slack channel to share the lessons from our failures. I sent a message to my organization, making it clear that I don't expect perfection. I shared my vision that we become a learning organization in town halls and one-on-ones.

Fail-safe architecture

Monoliths are natural when building a new company or when you have a small team. Monoliths are simple to make and more straightforward to deploy when you don't have multiple teams building together. As the codebase and organization grow, microservices become a better model.

It is critical to recognize when a monolith is becoming a challenge instead of an enabler. Microservices require a lot more infrastructure to support them. In addition, the effort to transition from one architecture to another is significant, so it is best to prepare before the need becomes urgent.

Avvo had already started moving to a microservices architecture, but a lack of investment stalled the transition. So, I increased investment in the infrastructure team. As a result, the team built tools that simplified creating, testing, monitoring, and deploying services. We then made rapid progress.

We also redesigned our organization[22] to leverage the reverse Conway Maneuver[23], further accelerating the new architecture.

YOU CAN BUILD A FAIL-SAFE / FAIL-SMART TEAM

In every company, I use the lessons I have shared in this article to build a culture where teams can innovate and learn from their users. It manifests differently with each group, but every team adopting these ideas has improved business outcomes and employee satisfaction. Work with your peers to adopt some of these ideas. Start small and grow. The process of adopting these concepts mirrors the product development process you are working to build.

If you decide it isn't a good fit for your company, you will have failed smart by failing small.

I will leave you with a final thought from Henry Ford.

"Failure is simply the opportunity to begin again, this time more intelligently."

HENRY FORD

CHAPTER 2

The challenge of top-down change and the Microsoft layoffs

Originally published on July 18, 2014

In my talks on engineering culture, I often discuss how to improve an existing culture or fix a broken one. I advocate for a bottom-up approach for large organizations to create actual culture change.

I have a few reasons for this:

1. Individual contributors or first-level managers are frequently my primary audience. I want to give them tools they can use to affect change in their larger organizations.
2. Bottom-up change takes longer, but it is more likely to be genuinely transformative. Moreover, because the whole

organization invests (eventually), it has a better chance of long-term success.

3. In a large organization, when a cultural change (or any kind of disruptive change) is pushed from senior leadership down, it tends to fail because the middle managers have usually attained their position by being successful in the old culture. This success bias makes them less likely to embrace change and more likely to only go through the motions while actively managing up to make it seem like they are participating.

Almost every time I advocate this bottom-up approach, I get a question asking if top-down change can also be effective. Sometimes this comes from a senior executive looking to lead change in the organization.[24]

When Steve Ballmer was trying to turn Microsoft's culture from competitive to cooperative with his "One Microsoft[25]" plan, I would claim that the chance of it succeeding was nearly zero for the third reason I mentioned above. Having worked at Microsoft in the 90s and early 2000s, I know the culture through which many of the then-Microsoft executives and middle management rose. Microsoft spent decades building a highly competitive culture. A restructure and top-down initiatives to encourage collaboration were unlikely to reverse decades of competition.

I pointed to the approach Marissa Meyer took at Yahoo as having a better chance of success. Yahoo was implementing new review policies[26] that seemed harsh to many in the company. These new review policies arrived with "silent layoffs," a significant effort to eliminate people in the company who were uninterested in the new culture. While this seemed unreasonably severe, it made a clear point: this was the new culture, and there was no tolerance for the old way of working.

In the memo that Satya Nadella sent to Microsoft[27] on July 18, 2014, outlining the layoffs that he was undertaking, one section caught my eye:

> In addition, we plan to have fewer layers of management, both top-down and sideways, to accelerate the flow of information and decision-making. This includes flattening organizations and increasing the span of control of people managers. In addition, our business processes and support models will be more lean and efficient with greater trust between teams.

This strategy differed sharply from Steve Ballmer's approach to culture change. Coupled with the largest layoff in the company's history was a clear message that a central target was the company's management. Moreover, the layoff served to underline the seriousness of the change. Flattening hierarchies and removing managers would eliminate or weaken those most likely to fight the cultural shift.

I think this has a much better chance for success than the One Microsoft approach, but it is still not guaranteed. Changing how 100,000 people approach their jobs is an hugely difficult task, after all.

The "house cleaning" approach may be a successful tactic in affecting cultural change in a large organization, but it is also perilous. The morale implications are significant. It would be most effective in a "do or die" situation where drastic action is necessary to save the company.

There is an argument that Yahoo was in this position when Marissa Meyer joined the company. From the folks I know at Yahoo, the aftermath of the shakeup produced a feeling of confidence and hope for the future.

Microsoft is not in a dire situation. While many in the industry and the press see the company sliding into irrelevancy, it is still amazingly profitable. This radical restructuring combined with layoffs may be greeted with significantly less enthusiasm from the employees. Satya Nadella may be taking advantage of his honeymoon period here, and that may be the thing that saves this.

I will continue to follow the progress of both leaders and companies as they try to evolve. It will be fascinating and instructive.

I hope they are successful for the Microsoft and Yahoo employees' sake.

Update

The changes at Yahoo were not enough to save the company's position in the industry, and Marissa Meyer is no longer the CEO.

My friends at Microsoft tell me that the company culture has changed significantly from the Gates/Ballmer era under Satya Nadella.

Career Development

The biggest career mistake I have seen technologists make is not having a destination or goal in mind. When you are just starting, learning the industry, it makes sense. If you reach the midpoint of your career and are not choosing roles based on a strategy, however, you may find yourself stuck in career limbo, trying to understand why your former peers are now your VP or architect.

I made that mistake myself, taking roles based on how much fun they sounded or what technologies I could play with rather than based on how they helped me achieve a career goal.

This section covers some lessons I have learned since I became more thoughtful about my career.

Taking a thoughtful approach to the job search process

Originally published on November 2, 2020

Does starting a job search fill you with fear? Have you taken roles in the past that you've regretted?

When a recruiter or interviewer asks, 'What are you looking for?' do you draw a blank?

I've been working long enough to have been through dozens of job interview loops. While I think I am pretty good at the process, I have still found myself not ready to answer the 'What do you want from your next role?' question.

I've also been a hiring manager long enough to have performed hundreds of interviews and seen all levels of answers to similar questions.

I completed a new job search in October 2020. Based on my past interviews and previous job decisions, and some frightening moments in my early interviews, I decided to take a more formal approach this time. I often talk and write about being deliberate and thoughtful in my decisions as a leader, so I thought I should take my own advice.

I created the following process to help me in my job search:

- Identify the things that were important to me in a job;
- Prioritize the criteria that I identified;
- Figure out how I could evaluate a potential position against my prioritized criteria.

IDENTIFYING WHAT WAS IMPORTANT

To make my list of criteria, I used a digital whiteboard tool and listed anything I thought was important in a job to me. Each idea went on a separate card (real cards would work fine too). Writing them down on paper might be tempting, but you must reorganize and group them. I would absolutely recommend cards or sticky notes (or their virtual equivalent) for this process. After my brainstorming, I had something that looked like this:

Figure 11 - My role criteria

The vertical and horizontal ordering had no specific meaning beyond a primitive affinity-grouping exercise[28] as I created the cards. I am sharing mine with you, but you should figure out your criteria since it is very personal.

PRIORITIZING

My next step was to sort each criterion based on how important it felt to me. After sorting, my cards looked like this:

Figure 12 - My prioritized criteria

Things in the same row were close in priority. I also sorted cards from left to right.

Then I color-coded them to help me understand the 'big picture' themes.

Figure 13 - Color-coded priorities

Now I had some helpful information about myself and what I wanted. Some things were surprising to me. Some things I had thought were essential weren't nearly as much of a priority when forcibly rated against others.

I learned that the company culture and mission are the most important things to me. After culture and mission are my role responsibilities, compensation/benefits, co-workers, the product, company stage, and finally, the tech stack.

ENTER THE SPREADSHEET

At this point, I realized that given my new strict prioritization, I could rate an opportunity against these criteria more objectively.

I exported my notes into a CSV file and loaded them into a spreadsheet. For each criterion, I added a quick explanation (so I would understand what I meant when I looked at it later). Then, I decided if it was a 'must-have,' and I assigned a score in decreasing order based on the ranking I had done. For each criterion, there was a simple Yes or No answer. Forcing a definitive decision requires you to make a choice instead of giving partial credit.

Each criterion can have a negative, zero, or positive score. The score is negative if the principle is a must-have, but the role does not meet it. The score is zero if the criterion is not a must-have, and the position does not meet it. The score is positive if the role meets the principle. Note that not all the 'must-haves' are the top priorities!

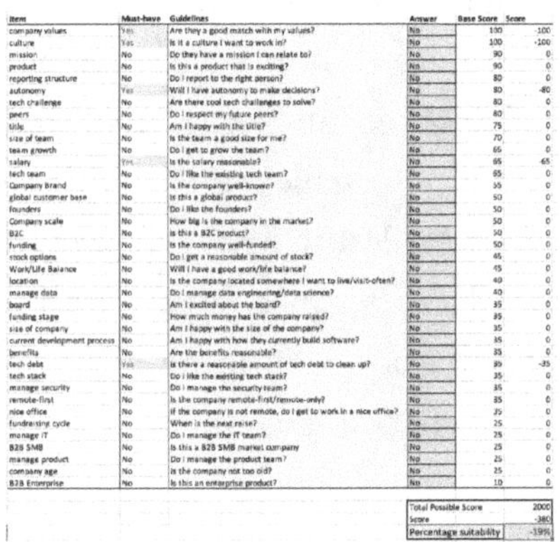

Item	Must-have	Guidelines	Answer	Base Score	Score
company values	Yes	Are they a good match with my values?	No	100	-100
culture	Yes	Is it a culture I want to work in?	No	100	-100
mission	No	Do they have a mission I can relate to?	No	90	0
product	No	Is this a product that is exciting?	No	90	0
reporting structure	No	Do I report to the right person?	No	80	0
autonomy	Yes	Will I have autonomy to make decisions?	No	80	-80
tech challenge	No	Are there cool tech challenges to solve?	No	80	0
peers	No	Do I respect my future peers?	No	80	0
title	No	Am I happy with the title?	No	75	0
size of team	No	Is the team a good size for me?	No	70	0
team growth	No	Do I get to grow the team?	No	65	0
salary	Yes	Is the salary reasonable?	No	65	-65
tech team	No	Do I like the existing tech team?	No	65	0
Company Brand	No	Is the company well-known?	No	55	0
global customer base	No	Is this a global product?	No	50	0
founders	No	Do I like the founders?	No	50	0
Company scale	No	How big is the company in the market?	No	50	0
B2C	No	Is this a B2C product?	No	50	0
funding	No	Is the company well-funded?	No	50	0
stock options	No	Do I get a reasonable amount of stock?	No	45	0
Work/Life Balance	No	Will I have a good work/life balance?	No	45	0
location	No	Is the company located somewhere I want to live/visit-often?	No	40	0
manage data	No	Do I manage data engineering/data science?	No	40	0
board	No	Am I excited about the board?	No	35	0
funding stage	No	How much money has the company raised?	No	35	0
size of company	No	Am I happy with the size of the company?	No	35	0
current development process	No	Am I happy with how they currently build software?	No	35	0
benefits	No	Are the benefits reasonable?	No	35	0
tech debt	Yes	Is there a reasonable amount of tech debt to clean up?	No	35	-35
tech stack	No	Do I like the existing tech stack?	No	35	0
manage security	No	Do I manage the security team?	No	35	0
remote-first	No	Is the company remote-first/remote-only?	No	35	0
nice office	No	If the company is not remote, do I get to work in a nice office?	No	35	0
fundraising cycle	No	When is the next raise?	No	25	0
manage IT	No	Do I manage the IT team?	No	25	0
B2B SMB	No	Is this a B2B SMB market company	No	25	0
manage product	No	Do I manage the product team?	No	25	0
company age	No	Is the company not too old?	No	25	0
B2B Enterprise	No	Is this an enterprise product?	No	10	0

Total Possible Score	2000
Score	-380
Percentage suitability	-19%

Figure 14 - Criteria in a spreadsheet

I made the total of the scores 2000 because that is a nice round number. Additionally, maintaining a target total forced me to decrease some scores if I wanted to raise others, another definitive decision.

I then reviewed my past few jobs and used the spreadsheet to compare them against the criteria. This process wasn't going to be completely objective. For example, rating a job I was in eight years ago against my current standards wouldn't be a completely effective measure of the role. But it let me do some 'sense checking' against my criteria and forced me to think a bit harder about some of them, which slightly adjusted the scores. After that exercise, I could look at each job's score to see if it seemed fitting, given my experience. While none of them were perfect, they each felt 'close enough' to a point where I was reasonably happy with the scoring.

Rating my previous roles against my current criteria also allowed me to look across them to find patterns and give me more insights about myself.

It was interesting to note that while my excitement about the product is central, I have only been excited about three of the last five products I worked on before I started the job. While having a good technology challenge is vital, I similarly only felt that in about three of my last five roles. I learned that while each is important, other factors can compensate for its lack. I also know that I am quite good at finding things about a product that can excite me, so that isn't as much of a concern to me as it would seem.

CREATING INTERVIEW QUESTIONS

For each of my criteria, I created a set of sample questions that I could use to help me evaluate a job. Given that my initial list of criteria was 39 items long, the list of questions ended up spanning five pages. I did not expect answers to all of these questions from an interviewer. Instead, the questions were prompts to help me think of ways to evaluate the company in an interview situation. I knew that if I did my due diligence in the interview process, I could answer any of those questions for the company.

The process was analogous to building interview questions for hiring someone in a company. You start with your company values or career ladder benchmarks and use them to generate questions for a candidate. My tenets list came from my prioritization exercise, and now I was developing the queries I needed to answer so that I could figure out how to score the role against them.

As I interviewed with different companies, I had the question prompts in front of me. If you have ever been in an interview, and the interviewer asks you, 'Do you have any questions for me?' and you can't think of anything immediately, having five pages of questions in your eye line is very helpful!

As I went through the interview processes, I reviewed my notes for each company to decide how comfortable I was rating them against my criteria. In some cases, I requested a couple of extra conversations to ensure I had a minimum confidence level.

MAKING A DECISION

Once I got to an offer stage, having my ratings was valuable in evaluating the specific offer and deciding if I wanted to extend the process to get to the offer stage with one of the other companies I was interviewing with. While there were a few companies I was excited about, my ratings made it clear that one company was the best fit for me. When we negotiated an offer I was happy with, I confidently accepted it.

DOING THIS YOURSELF

If this process seems like something you want to employ, I can recommend it, but it is worth understanding the limitations.

This process gave me a sense of objectivity, but it is still subjective.

My feelings about my past jobs are all colored by my experiences working at them for years. Had I used this process when I interviewed, would I have predicted how the role would have turned out accurately? Probably not, although I might have focused more on specific areas in the interview process. If I ever leave my new job, it will be worth doing this exercise again for the company to see how my feelings changed over my tenure.

My ability to judge an opportunity against 39 criteria during an interview round of some hours will always be suspect. In addition, there will always be some bias based on my experience during the interview process.

You must be very careful when creating your list of criteria not to fall victim to social desirability bias[29]. For example, are the items in the list things you care about or something you think you should care about? The prioritization process can help with this, but it is still an easy trap.

My evaluation of my past roles showed that my favorite jobs only satisfied around 80% of my criteria. This result seemed a bit off (even adjusting for the 'what I want now' vs. the 'what I wanted then' bias). I was least happy with the roles that were less than 60% of a match. While the percentage matches weren't perfect in absolute numbers, they were different enough in relative numbers for me to be comfortable with my criterion. I rescanned my priorities to see if they resulted from social desirability bias. Still, I think it was my criterion evolving based on my experiences.

While there are some limitations to the objectivity of the process, I found building my criteria, generating questions based on them, and evaluating my past roles extremely valuable. It made me think about what I wanted at this career stage and what I appreciated and disliked about my former positions. In addition, this exercise helped me be much more self-aware when talking to recruiters and people at each company.

Thanks to this process, I was able to cut short interview loops when it became apparent that the job wouldn't meet my criteria. I could say no to jobs that I might have otherwise interviewed for in the past. When I found the proper role for me, I accepted it without fear of missing out on another position.

While you may not want to create as formal of a process as I did when looking for a new role, if you take one thing away from this chapter, let it be that it is worth spending some time to think through your past positions, where you want to go in your career, and what is important to you in a job. Having that self-awareness in an interview process will give you a better sense of the questions you are trying to answer and a higher confidence level when you interview.

CHAPTER 4

When, why, and how to stop coding as your day job

By letting go of writing code, you open yourself up to excelling as a manager.

Originally published on March 12, 2021

I AM A COMPUTER PROGRAMMER.

I was one of those people who started coding at a young age – in my case, on a TRS-80 Model 1 in my school's library. I loved teaching the computer to do something and then enjoying the results of interacting with what I built. Since I didn't own a computer, I would fill spiral-bound notebooks with programs I would write at home. Then, as soon as I could get time on the computer, I would type it in line by line. When I learned that I could write software as a job, I couldn't imagine anything else I would want to do.

After graduating from university, I got my dream job writing 3D graphics code. I was a software engineer! I defined a successful day by how much code I wrote, the compiler issues I resolved, and the bugs I closed. These were obvious, objective metrics that I could use to measure my work. Those metrics and my job defined me.

Today, I am a Chief Technology Officer, leading large software development organizations. If I am writing code on the product, it is probably a bad thing. I now have to define my success by much fuzzier metrics: building good teams, hiring and training good people, setting multi-year technical strategy and vision for the company, collaborating with other departments, and setting and managing a budget. I may have a good or bad day, but I must measure my success based on quarters or years.

My achievements are now always tied to the successes of others. Getting to this point wasn't easy, but I wouldn't have it any other way. The journey took years. The first challenge was understanding that coding was no longer my job.

WHY IS IT HARD TO STOP CODING AS OUR DAY-TO-DAY WORK?

When I speak to engineering leads or managers working to grow into more senior engineering leadership levels, the question of 'How much do you code?' is very often raised. We usually have a hard time imagining that we can still be useful if we don't code for a significant part of our time. Why is that?

We've been traditionally bad at hiring managers in the software engineering industry

Usually, companies choose development leads because they are the best, technically, on the team. I would guess that the reasoning behind this is the assumption that the best developers are the right people to supervise their peers. Unfortunately, this practice creates the impression that managing others is a promotion for a skilled developer when, in actuality, it is a career change away from what made them successful in the first place.

The worst managers I've had were very talented developers who hated spending time doing the "boring" stuff that wasn't coding. They resented the time spent away from the keyboard and weren't always good at hiding that fact.

Many companies now feature dual career tracks for technologists, allowing them to advance as individual contributors or move into management. This choice of career is an excellent thing. It means that if you want to spend your days coding, you can do that without sacrificing your career. It also means that if you prefer to find your joy in leading teams and growing others' development and skills, you can do that.

We fear becoming 'non-technical'

We joined the technology industry to be close to technology. We fear that by moving away from coding, we will morph into the classic 'pointy-haired boss' – ridiculed by the people on our team and unable to understand what the developers are discussing. I won't say this can't happen, but it won't happen on its own. It will only happen if you avoid technology once you move into management.

As you take on broader leadership responsibilities, you must learn and understand new technologies. Moving beyond the specifics of your expertise is necessary to move up in management. I have managed developers coding in at least a dozen languages on the backend, frontend, mobile, operating systems, and native applications. I have also managed testers, data scientists, data engineers, DevOps, Security, designers, data analysts, program managers, product managers, corporate IT teams, and others. It isn't possible to be an expert in all those fields. I need to take the lessons from my time as a developer and use them to inform my understanding, help me learn new areas, and give me empathy for the people who work for me.

It isn't that you will become non-technical. It is that you will become *less narrowly technical.*

As new managers, we are often expected to continue coding

It is common to move from being a developer on a team to managing that team. As the new manager, this means you are still responsible for part of the codebase. Unless you immediately start leading a large group, your new role may require you to spend a significant portion of your time coding. This expectation makes the transition to the new role more comfortable – but it can also be an anchor that holds you back from embracing your new role as your management responsibilities grow.

We still see ourselves as a resource that can 'save' a deliverable

As a manager, you are accountable for the results of your team. If the group struggles to make a deadline, it might be tempting to jump into the weeds to try and help the team finish the project on time. While this is sometimes the right decision, it can also worsen the problems because the team loses the person who looks at the more significant issues and coordinates with other teams to get more help or prepare them for the delay.

WHY DO WE NEED TO STOP CODING EVENTUALLY?

We don't need to stop coding, ever. However, once you move into engineering leadership, it will need to become a smaller and smaller part of your job if you are working to lead larger teams or broaden your responsibilities.

I had led teams before I was a manager at Adobe, and I had always spent a significant part of my work week contributing code as part of the groups I was in. At Adobe, though, my team had grown to be fourteen people, with another four dotted-lined to me.

I had been the primary developer for a part of the project, and I still took pride in contributing important features to every release. However, my management responsibilities were starting to fill my work weeks. Between 1:1s, sync meetings with other teams, and other manager work, my feature development time was increasingly moving into my evenings and weekends. As a result, my features were often the last to be merged and usually late.

The company had two mandatory shut-down weeks. To work during this time, you needed the prior approval of a Vice-President. The team was preparing for a release, and my features were still in the to-do column; I met with my VP to get his permission to work over the shut-down week. He asked me, 'Who is the worst developer on your team?' I hemmed and hawed – I didn't want to call out anyone on my team, and I hadn't even considered the question. Finally, seeing my uncertainty, he answered for me. 'You are! You're always late with your features. The rest of the team is always waiting on you. If you were a developer instead of the manager, you would be on a performance improvement plan.' He was right. My insistence on coding was hurting the team, not helping it.

Taking on the lead role doesn't mean you should stop coding immediately, but it does mean that your coding responsibilities should now be secondary to your leadership ones. Other developers are on your team, but there aren't other leads. If you aren't doing your lead job, no one else will. Similarly, your professional development's primary focus should now be your leadership skills, not your coding skills. You are moving into a new career, and if you don't work to improve, you will find yourself stuck.

As your leadership responsibilities increase, you should transition your development responsibilities to other team members. This transition is good practice because **delegation is an essential part of leadership.**

HOW DO YOU STAY 'TECHNICAL' WHEN CODING IS NO LONGER YOUR JOB?

As I said earlier, staying technical is a choice you must make. Hopefully, one of the primary reasons you chose to make a career in the technology industry was that you were interested in it, so this shouldn't be a problem.

As I also said earlier, as you develop as a technology leader, your focus broadens as your scope widens.

The best way that I have found to remain a credible technologist for my teams is to be interested in them and their work. To do this, talk to the team members and take a genuine interest in their work. If a technology comes up in a meeting or 1:1 that you don't know, add it to a list of things to research later. Then, dedicate time in your week to go through that list and learn about the technologies on your list well enough to have your own opinions about them. This practice allows you to have further discussions with whoever mentioned the technology.

If you get interested in what you learn about the new technology, you may want to keep trying to understand it better; you may read more or embark on a personal project using it to gain more practical knowledge. As I said, it isn't that you must stop coding. It is that, eventually, it shouldn't be your day job anymore.

By taking an interest in the technologies your team uses in their work, you deepen your empathy for them and expand your knowledge. You'll be able to discuss the work, ask reasonable questions, and make connections to other things happening in the organization and your own experience. This way, the people on your team know that while you may not be able to step in for them, you understand their work and care about it.

SUCCESS IS DEFINED DIFFERENTLY WHEN YOU LEAD PEOPLE

The feeling of accomplishment that comes from completing a cool user story, deploying a new service, or fixing a difficult bug is significant. It is a dopamine hit, and just like other dopamine-inducing behaviors, it can be hard to stop.

Having a great 1:1 or leading a productive team meeting can also feel good but in a more esoteric way. As a team leader, you must learn to perceive the success of making others successful.

This type of success takes longer, but the feeling is more profound and more rewarding.

Having a release resonate with your customers, being able to easily justify the promotion of a developer you have mentored, and having someone accept a job offer for your team, are all fantastic feelings. In the day-to-day, watching stories get completed, helping resolve the issues when they aren't, and seeing people get excited about the direction you're setting for the team can leave you feeling satisfied at the end of the day.

BEING A TECHNICAL LEADER DOESN'T MEAN WRITING CODE EVERY DAY

As you grow in your new leadership career, you must devote time to mentoring, developing, and leading your team. As you spend less time in your code editor, you will find new challenges in strategy, clearing roadblocks, fixing broken processes, and new tools like HR information systems, slides, and spreadsheets (it isn't as bad as it sounds). You will spend less time learning all the intricacies of a specific language or toolchain. Instead, you will learn about how systems interact, understand when to build vs. buy, and learn about new technology areas. And you can still code, but make sure you aren't the developer holding your team back.

CHAPTER 5

The Personal Strategy Off-site

Originally published on May 3, 2020

THE WHIRLWIND

In the whirlwind of day-to-day work, it is often hard to carve out time for something that does not have a specific deliverable. Working from home can be even more challenging because of the additional pressures of helping your family. A familiar dictum of strategic thinking is the criticality of taking the time to think and plan.

THE PERSONAL STRATEGY DAY

Liminal spaces are the transitionary spaces between things. In the liminal space between working from home to being back fully in the office environment, you can try something new—a personal strategy day.

Block out a day in your calendar as people return to the office. There will be some turbulence then as everyone is transitioning. It is the perfect time to start thinking about what you want to accomplish for yourself and your team before the whirlwind begins again.

THE PERSONAL OFF-SITE

Companies schedule off-sites to get away from the distractions of the office. If you can find a "third place" (a place that is not your office or your home) where you can focus, that is ideal. If not, book a secluded conference room in your office, or find an empty desk far from where you usually sit. If you are still at home, let your family know you are working and need some blocks of focused time.

FOCUS

Don't read your e-mail. Don't take any meetings. Your job on that day is to think and plan. To help me focus, I usually print out supporting materials and work on paper to avoid the lure of notifications and other electronic distractions. Think of this as a gift of time and focus that you are giving yourself.

Figure 15 - My preparation for my personal strategy off-site

WHAT TO CONSIDER

Think of the time before the lockdowns began. You may have just been starting on your 2020 commitments and deliverables. What was going well then? What were your concerns? Now think through what you have learned about your team, the work, and yourself during the lockdown. What do you want to keep, and what do you want to discard as you return to the office? What is it about the industry you are in and the world at large that has changed? What new pitfalls and opportunities are there? Now think ahead to the rest of the year. What new goals should you have for yourself and your team?

Take notes. Write things down. You will want to refer to them as you go through the year to revisit or remind yourself of your thinking.

Now create a plan. Not too detailed because the world is going to keep changing. Detailed enough, you feel you have something against which to execute. Write that down, also with milestones, if possible.

Finally, think about the process you just completed. Did it work for you? Would you do it again? If so, what would you change next time?

RETROSPECT AND REVISIT

This process may take anywhere from a couple of hours to an entire day. Don't be too preoccupied with the length of time you spend. You are starting to build a practice of taking time for strategic thinking, so this is about taking more time than you have before.

If you find this valuable, you may want to plan your next strategy day for six or twelve months from now. Again, block it out in the calendar early and protect that time!

You may also find that scheduling smaller blocks of time, weekly or monthly, is suitable for revisiting your plan, tracking progress, and adjusting. These blocks of time are strategic thinking too!

CONCLUSION

Building a structured approach like a personal strategy day may help you create a practice if you struggle to keep time for strategy. Using the liminal times, like transitioning from lockdown back to whatever comes after, is an opportunity to block and protect time. The liminal times are also crucial for strategy because your past assumptions are likely no longer correct, and there may be some opportunities or challenges that weren't visible before.

SOME RESOURCES

I've spent the last several years building a structured personal strategy process for myself. So many people have inspired my practice. Their suggestions may inspire you as well.

- When I worked at Microsoft, I always remembered the lead-up to Bill Gates' Think Weeks and the output from them. It was an amazing practice: https://www.cnbc.com/2019/07/26/bill-gates-took-solo-think-weeks-in-a-cabin-in-the-woods.html
- This talk from Maria Gutierrez at the Lead Dev conference was a massive help in my strategic planning. https://www.youtube.com/watch?v=4pa6G23ygp0
- The planners from the Ink+Volt team helped me build some structure around my strategy and plan regular times to revisit and update it. Kate Matsudaira provides useful, structured planning and strategic thinking documents in her newsletter and on their blog. https://inkandvolt.com/blogs/articles
- In Pat Kua's LevelUp newsletter, the issues near the end and the start of the year included many planning and

strategy resources. https://levelup.patkua.com/#archive

CHAPTER 6

Own your calendar

Originally published on July 20, 2021

Every six months, I take a day to review and reflect on how things have been going and the changes I want to make moving forward. This day is my personal strategy off-site.

As part of the process, I think about what I want to do more of, what I want to do less of, and how much time I should allocate each week toward my professional goals. I then create a sample of what a perfect day would look like and a mockup of what an ideal week would look like apportioning my time in alignment with my goals.

With my review and planning done, I go to my work calendar and clean it up to make it look like my ideal week. I delete or stop attending meetings that are not useful. I block out time for focused work on my goals. Then, to give some flexibility for the things that arise, I make sure that I leave some gaps or mark some of my project-work time as "free," allowing others to schedule it if needed.

Each week has unique challenges: unforeseen work appears, a critical customer meeting dominates, or a work emergency takes over my calendar.

At the end of the week, I look back at the calendar and figure out how much of my time spent maps to my planned time allocation.

Often, I find that new things are creeping in if I am not attentive. As my time diverges from my ideal allocation, I must decide if I change my plan based on my new reality (and possibly adjust my goals) or re-assert my plan and delegate or drop the new constraints on my time.

I track each week's time allocations in a spreadsheet. It helps me understand where I am spending my time over the year. In addition, it makes it very clear if I am spending too much time on low-value work. The spreadsheet also shows if I am unrealistic about how I allocate my time in a week which is helpful for the next six-month planning.

This process may seem very rigid, and in many ways, it is. However, I've come to it over the years through iteration after finding myself feeling very busy but not making meaningful progress toward my personal or professional goals.

As we grow in our roles, new opportunities and responsibilities appear. Our peers, team, and others want our input and time. This activity gives us the impression that we are doing necessary, valuable work. We may look at our full calendars at the end of the week and wonder what we accomplished. If this situation feels familiar to you, it may be worth adding some rigor to understand how you want to spend your time and how you actually spend your time.

CHAPTER 7

In 2018 Decide to Work Deliberately

Originally published on January 1, 2018

"I went to the woods because I wished to live deliberately, to front only the essential facts of life, and see if I could not learn what it had to teach, and not, when I came to die, discover that I had not lived."

HENRY DAVID THOREAU

You may have heard this quote before. Maybe it resonated with you, or maybe not. What does it mean to live (and work) deliberately?

I've thought a lot about this over the last few years.

Earlier in my career, I certainly wasn't deliberate. I "went with my gut" a lot. Some of it was my lack of experience, and some was an overinflated ego.

As I got more experience, I looked back at earlier decisions that I had made as a leader and realized how poorly considered some of them were. I could have put myself and my team in a much better position with more thought. I've also been lucky enough to work with people who have modeled what approaching work thoughtfully can look like.

Consider all the decisions you make in a day at your job. You work on this project instead of that one. You choose the opening phrase you make in your pitch to a customer. You attend this training or decide to skip it. You invite one colleague to lunch and not another. You hire this person instead of that one. How much thought do you put into each of these decisions? Do you know why you made this choice? Do you ever evaluate what worked well or poorly and what you might do differently the next time?

Some of these decisions might seem obvious in the moment. Next time you encounter a decision that appears trivial, take a beat, and just think about why the choice is so clear. Every choice you make means that you are also choosing not to do something. Have you considered both options? Every decision is the start of a chain of events. What are the assumptions you are making about the effects of this choice? Later, return to your decision and test if your assumptions were correct. Was it still the best option? What did you learn from this that you will bring forward?

Thinking strategically is thinking through your assumptions and the implications of a decision and evaluating the outcome.

Being strategic is critical for big company decisions but is also valuable in the decisions you make all day.

It does take a bit of practice to do this, but as with anything you practice, it gets easier. It will eventually become second nature.

So, next time you make a hiring decision or decide to work on project X tomorrow so you can do project Y today, ask yourself, "Why is this the right thing to do?" If you can't answer immediately, spend a minute and consider. You may realize that it isn't the right choice, and the next time you may spend more time making that decision.

> "Look at every path closely and deliberately, then ask ourselves this crucial question: Does this path have a heart? If it does, then the path is good. If it doesn't, it is of no use."
>
> CARLOS CASTANEDA

CHAPTER 8

How I Get My Focused Work Done

Originally published on May 31, 2018

In management, we can become very "interrupt driven." We get so used to distractions that we count on them. This dependency can make it very hard to focus when we need to. My calendar fills up with meetings. My unscheduled time is full of people stopping by to ask questions or chat. If I am not careful, I will find myself doing a lot of work at night.

I've tried many ways to improve my focused time over the years. Here are the things that work best for me.

DEFRAG YOUR CALENDAR

Every six months, I review my schedule. Recurring meetings tend to accumulate over time. This periodic review makes it easier to identify meetings that are no longer necessary. I also will try to reschedule my recurring meetings so that they group into blocks. Those 30 minutes or an hour between meetings are a waste of time. It isn't enough time to work on anything significant. Grouping my meetings gives me larger blocks of time that I can use for focused work.

BLOCK OUT YOUR FOCUSED AND LOOSELY STRUCTURED TIME

Now that your calendar has larger blocks of time, add recurring calendar entries to protect parts of your week for focused work. I need at least two hours to engage in a task, so I don't block out less than that. Ideally, I will block out more.

Putting it on the calendar discourages other people from scheduling you at that time. Likewise, I also block out time for unstructured work, like reading e-mails. Reading e-mails or returning phone calls works well in those one-hour blocks between meetings. Having dedicated unstructured time also means less temptation to do unstructured work in my focused blocks.

Make sure you leave some gaps in your schedule to allow folks to add in a meeting if needed. I made the mistake of filling my calendar almost entirely for a while. As a result, people started to ignore my free/busy time because they couldn't find any empty meeting slots.

SET OUT A "DO NOT DISTURB" FLAG

In an open-plan environment, create a sign so people know not to disturb you.

I have a weird lamp on my desk. People know that I am trying to concentrate when the light is on. For the most part, they will let me focus. When I worked in an office, I would put a post-it on my door with a note asking people to send me an e-mail unless it was urgent.

GET OUT OF THE BUILDING

Sometimes to focus, you need to go elsewhere. For example, I will sometimes go to a nearby cafe, co-working space, or library if I need a few uninterrupted hours.

TURN OFF THE NOTIFICATIONS

There is a reason that you see this advice shared often. I turn on "Do Not Disturb" on my computer and phone. I have a separate Chrome "Person" with only the extensions I need for focused work and no notifications enabled. I quit all apps that are not the ones I need for my task. My phone goes into my pocket. I don't want any electronic distractions.

If I must write something, I will sometimes do it longhand on paper first to eliminate distractions. Writing on paper works exceptionally well for me if it isn't a topic I am excited about but need to get done. Also, once I have the first draft on paper, it is much easier to edit and refine it on the computer without being tempted to do something else.

SET A GOAL AND REWARD YOURSELF

We are so unfocused these days that gamifying your focused work may help. For example, when I finish the first draft of this post, I will spend 10 minutes on Twitter to reward myself for getting it done without interruptions.

SET ASIDE A WHOLE DAY FOR YOUR FOCUSED WORK

It is sometimes challenging for a manager to have an entire day clear. If I have something vital to do, especially something time sensitive, I will clear the whole day to focus on it. Usually, I will also get out of the building to avoid other work distractions. I give myself a one-person off-site to get something done. I turn on my "out of office" e-mail responder with a note letting people know that I am working off-site and asking them not to disturb me unless it is critical. I will also schedule these "focus days" up to a quarter in advance to ensure I have them in case I want to use them.

CLEAN YOUR DESK

Cleaning the clutter in your eye-line is also very common and helpful advice. Things accumulate on my desk: mail, tchotchkes, magazines, books. When you are trying to focus, they can be distractions, or the general clutter can be a distraction. You don't need to clean your desk thoroughly. You just don't need to see that stuff. Put it all somewhere you can't see when trying to focus.

CLEAN YOUR COMPUTER DESKTOP

Just like your physical environment can be a distraction, your virtual one can be too. All those files on your desktop are like an extensive to-do list of fun things instead of the work you need to focus on. So, create a "clutter" folder and move everything into it.

CREATE YOUR FOCUSED PLAYLIST

Some people like to work in silence. I find that music helps me focus better, especially in busy environments. Different playlists help me focus on reading, programming, and writing. For reading, I like ambient music. For programming, it is post-rock and electronic music. When writing, I favor modern classical music.

You may prefer silence, or music may help you. One important thing for me is that the music on my playlists is music I know well. Listening to new music can be too distracting for me in these situations.

START WITH A MINDFULNESS EXERCISE

Especially on my focus days, I like to start with a ten or twenty-minute mindfulness exercise to help me clear away the other things on my mind and help me focus on the task at hand.

MAKE YOUR EXHAUSTIVE TO-DO LIST

One of the exercises I like from the *Getting Things Done* book by David Allen is exhaustively writing down everything you need to do. It is very freeing for me. I find that if I need to remember to do something, it will nag at me the whole time I am trying to focus. So if I write it down on paper or in a to-do app, it helps me put it aside for a while so I can concentrate.

CHAPTER 9

The Known Unknowns

Originally published on March 9, 2014

...there are known knowns; there are things we know that we know. There are known unknowns; that is to say, there are things that we now know we don't know. But there are also unknown unknowns – there are things we do not know we don't know.

DONALD RUMSFELD

Last week I held a day of training for the managers and folks interested in becoming managers in my organization. I did this with some of the folks from Spotify's excellent People Operations team, Paolo Brolin Echeverria and Mats Oldin.

As part of the exercises, we identified which management skills, values, and responsibilities were the most critical for our organization. We then did something like a spider map to help us evaluate our competencies in these areas and set goals on how we'd like to improve over the next few months. The exercises were fantastic, and they identified some genuinely great qualities of managers and leaders that I hadn't considered. I'll try and write about them in the future.

One thing that struck me as I did this self-assessment was how low I rated myself in some areas. Areas that my managers had told me that I was strong in. I rated myself low in spaces that I would even call my strengths. The reason was that I had come to realize how much better I could be than I am right now. I knew how much more I had to learn, my **known unknowns**.

I had noticed this before in other areas. For years, when I interviewed C++ developers, one of my favorite questions was, "how do you rate your C++ skill on a scale from 1 to 10?" Sometimes, I'd add the context of "1 is your dog, and 10 is Bjarne Stroustrup." I was looking for not an assessment of what they knew but an understanding of what they didn't know: the known unknowns. I wrote C++ code professionally every day for over 15 years, and I would have rated myself a 7 (and that was before C++11 came out). Anyone who rated themselves higher than that either was just not being honest (it was an interview situation, after all), or they knew so little of the language that they didn't have a clue how inexperienced they were.

I now realize that this is just part of mastery. You reach a plateau in your growth, and it seems like you are getting pretty good, but then you grow a bit more and realize there is so much more to learn—ad infinitum.

CHAPTER 10

Becoming a CTO

Originally published on November 1, 2021

A former co-worker reached out to me recently. They are a director of engineering at a midsize startup and just got their first headhunter inquiry for a CTO role. Having never been in the role before, they wanted to know what the position was like and how to prepare for the interviews.

I realized that while there are some books on technology leadership careers, there aren't many resources explaining the most senior levels. I will attempt to provide some insight and advice for those interested in someday becoming a CTO.

I'VE BEEN A CTO FOR FIVE AND A HALF YEARS

I've worked at a hundred-thousand-person company, seed-stage startups, and many of the variants in between. I started as a developer and followed a traditional path of moving up to more senior levels on the development track and then moving to lead, engineering manager, director, VP, and now chief technology officer. I've been the CTO at three different companies in two countries and three parts of the technology industry. I'm part of a few networks where I meet and talk with CTOs of all sizes and stages of companies.

I've learned that one reason there isn't a good reference for the role of the CTO is that the size of the company and the expectations of the CEO define the job. Some of my role expectations and responsibilities are like those of many of my peers at similar-size companies. However, there are also significant differences in the expectations from our executive peers and boards.

Because of the variability of the role, I will broadly share my direct experiences, joined with an understanding of the expectations of other CTOs that I know.

THE EARLY-STAGE COMPANY CTO IS OFTEN THE DEVELOPER-IN-CHIEF

At earlier-stage companies, the CTO is often the technical co-founder. They are likely the developer who built many of the earlier versions of the software and helped hire the original development team. Their responsibilities are primarily technical: driving architecture, doing advanced development tasks, and creating technical vision.

Frequently, the first CTO of the company is hired for their ability to code and not their ability to grow or manage a team. Depending on the person, they may also lead the development team. Still, often the team's management will eventually move to another person, an experienced manager, who may report to the CTO or be a peer to them.

The early-stage CTO is the leading technical voice for the company externally, especially if they are a co-founder. They talk to investors and potential partners and meet with potential vendors. If they also manage the development team, they will solely represent engineering in the senior leadership team. As a result, they will have responsibility for the decisions made by the engineering team. Nevertheless, if they do not manage the team directly, they might not be involved in the decisions around the day-to-day operations.

A mistake that inexperienced founding CTOs often make is that they don't understand their role beyond coder-in-chief. They focus solely on the technology and are not active participants in the company's leadership. As a result, they do not work cross-functionally. CTOs fixated on the how without the why or what will not be in the role very long once the company grows.

If they have no experience leading an engineering team or organization, the early-stage CTO will be challenged to grow with the company. If they cannot scale, eventually they will end up in a subordinate role reporting to a more experienced CTO hired to replace them.

THE MIDSIZE COMPANY CTO IS RESPONSIBLE FOR LEADING THE ORGANIZATION,

CORPORATE STRATEGY, AND MAKING TECHNICAL DECISIONS

Once a company reaches a size at which it needs new processes and structures, the scrappy leaders who helped get the company off the ground are often replaced with more experienced leaders knowledgeable in taking companies through the next growth stage. If the early-stage CTO hasn't grown into the larger role, they will be part of that replaced group.

The midsize company CTO is a full-fledged executive team member working cross-functionally and meeting with partners, investors, and customers. Frequently, the midsize company CTO will also manage the engineering organization. The CTO is responsible for setting technical direction, making sure good architectural decisions are being made, and establishing best practices and working methods. They are still expected to have good technical depth, but don't often actively contribute to shipping code. A red flag for me personally is seeing a CTO role description where the expectation is to lead a 50-plus-person organization while also actively coding on the product. It means the executive team does not have appropriate expectations for the role.

A midsize company CTO spends significant time establishing culture and practices for the teams they are responsible for; they are also very directly accountable for the organization's decisions and its track record of delivery. The CTO meets internally with members of the other functions, such as sales, marketing, HR, and finance, to share direction for the organization and get feedback. The CTO is responsible for the administration of the teams, including the budget.

The CTO is also responsible for hiring, performance management, and team structure—and may be very active in their teams' recruitment and interview processes, especially in a scale-up type of company.

A CTO leading a more extensive development organization must be a generalist, understanding different roles and responsibilities. Their remit may include Corporate IT and Technical Support. In some companies, they may also manage the business analytics, security, product, and UX teams. A CTO who is too focused on the areas closest to their background or does not respect non-coding functions will not succeed.

As a midsize company CTO, you will often spend as much time with your peers and their teams as you spend with your own. As a result, you will need to learn about their functions and how your teams can work together. CTOs who "stay in their lane" will not be seen as an equal member of the senior leadership team and may lose their say in decisions that affect the organization.

It is very unusual for someone to move into a midsize company CTO role without having some experience leading a multilevel-development organization and working with other business functions.

GROWING (OR MOVING) INTO THE CTO ROLE

If you are a manager or a manager of managers with the goal of being a CTO, there are a few things you can start to focus on that will help you on your path.

Learn about the business your company is in

Offer to sit in on sales calls, on user research interviews. Try to understand the company's financials when the CFO presents them. If you can't, make a friend in the finance team and ask them to explain them to you. Understand the Key Performance Indicators not only for your team, but also for the teams around you.

Learn about the other functions

Get recommendations of reading or conference talks from your peers in the product, UX, and marketing teams. Think about how their work influences yours, and vice-versa.

Respect and learn other technology areas aside from your own

If you lead an area you don't have personal experience in, approach the people in that function with respect and a genuine desire to understand their work. They want to help you know what they do and how they do it.

Hone your craft

Hopefully, you are already working on deepening your skill as an engineering manager or director, but are you trying to understand the bigger picture? Read other companies' (public) handbooks, engineering blog posts, and conference presentations about their ways of working. What practices are interesting?

Which can you try in your team? How do you think they will scale, or what issues do you think they may have?

Ask your CTO if there are tasks they can delegate to you

The best way to learn the job is to do the job. Even better is having someone who is already doing the job explain to you how they perform it so you can help them.

Start thinking in terms of strategy

The main difference between the expectations of line managers and senior managers is the emphasis on strategic thinking. Executives contribute to the company's strategic planning and use their understanding of the company's goals and the current situation to make sure that their teams are setting up the conditions for the company's success. Strategic thinking is a learnable skill, but it takes practice.

THE REWARDS OF BEING A CTO

Being a CTO was not what I imagined it to be when I first decided it was my career goal. It is a lot of work, carries much stress, has fewer perks than you might think, and can be somewhat lonely. However, it is also the most personally rewarding job I have ever had. With the challenges, there is also incredible responsibility, tons to learn, the ability to influence the company's direction, and the chance to affect the lives of dozens or hundreds of people on your team. I have yet to regret my choice to pursue this role.

Managing Teams

People often conflate the words "Managing" and "Leading." This conflation is incorrect. Individuals with no direct reports can be leaders, but managers are only managers because they are responsible for hiring, firing, and performance-managing their employees. Managers must balance the needs of their organization, the needs of their employees, and the requirements of organizational governance processes while delivering on company goals. It is challenging, and few organizations adequately prepare their new managers for their responsibilities.

CHAPTER 11

Building a vernacular with your engineering team

Originally published January 8, 2021

Teams consist of people. People communicate via a common language. The base unit of most languages is words.

THE IMPACT OF LANGUAGE

Whether written or spoken, words are essential – both the general terms we use and those specific to our work.

The terms and phrases that are specific to our jobs or our companies create a vernacular. The definition of vernacular according to Merriam-Webster is 'the mode of expression of a group or class.' Our vernacular separates software developers from lawyers, Amazon employees from Microsoft employees, and your team from the other teams in your company.

The words and phrases that we use in team discussions give us a shorthand. They save time. Instead of saying, 'Ok, deploy this to production, let the support team know that it is going live, and then let marketing know once it has gone to 50% of active users.' Your team may just say, 'let's deploy-ify it.' The larger context is defined and understood in the vernacular of your team.

One of the challenges of joining a new company or a new team is learning the vernacular. One of the significant struggles of team forming or cross-team communication is different definitions for the same words.

Consider the word 'Agile'. To you, it may mean 'Scrum' because your only experience working in Agile teams was working with the Scrum framework. For me, it may mean Kanban or a set of principles not tied to any specific framework. If we are on the same team and I say that I think we should work in an Agile way, we could have very different interpretations of what that means, which may inadvertently create tension in the team.

'Done' is another word that often leads to problems – both for a development lead and between teams. A developer on your team says that their feature is 'done'. Do they mean that they finished the code? That they tested the code? That they deployed it to the staging environment? That the code is running in production? That the A/B tests for the code have completed?

Having clarity on the meaning of words is critical. Companies will often create glossaries of the terms and phrases in everyday use to help onboard new employees. You should do the same for your team for the words and phrases your team uses day-to-day.

As a leader, you should also deliberately cultivate your team vernacular.

CREATING A TEAM VERNACULAR

Creating a team vernacular is a simple way to drive team unity, identity, and alignment around best practices.

A simple way to start building a team vernacular is to use a group meeting to identify and define the words and phrases used in the team. You can get the discussion started by spending a few weeks taking note of words or phrases that come up often in team discussions. Terms such as done, tested, shipped, agile, stuck, autonomy, microservice, or waiting, may have different definitions from different people on a team.

Ask the team what they think each of these words means. If there is a general agreement, add it to your team glossary. Don't stress over creating a perfect definition for each word. You can reference a dictionary definition or definitive blog post if you want, but your goal is team consensus around the meaning, nothing more.

Once the team establishes the primary vernacular, update it as necessary. Clarify the definitions of the new terms introduced. If someone uses a word in a new way, ask, 'What does that word mean to you?' If you don't recognize a term that others are using, ask the team for the definition. Add these new words and phrases to your glossary. Over time, the meanings of words will change as they understand new subtleties or gain new skills. When this happens, append or replace the existing definitions.

USING YOUR VERNACULAR TO TRAIN THE TEAM

Creating consistency in the words you use, or introducing new words, is also a valuable way to train your team or introduce new concepts.

You may find that there is debate within the team about the constraints for a system to be called a 'microservice'. This debate is an opportunity to find blog posts or a book for the team to read together and discuss to create the definition for the team glossary.

If you want to understand secure coding practices better, you could watch a conference talk as a team and then discuss what words and techniques you could introduce into your vernacular.

As you build your glossary, include the phrase and what it means to your team and the references your team used to arrive at that meaning. Your dictionary can then become an onboarding tool, a training tool, and a reference to share with other groups.

VERNACULARS HAPPEN

Groups of friends, co-workers, teams, and families all create unique vernaculars over time. The in-jokes you have with friends, the shorthand you have with your partner, the CEO's catch-phrase. Be aware of this, be deliberate about it within your team, and use this naturally occurring phenomenon to your advantage!

CHAPTER 12

The p-word

Originally published on September 9, 2021

I have never heard the word "politics" used in a positive light when describing a work situation. On the contrary, the words "corporate politics" evoke memories of cynical executives in '90s movies quoting **The Art of War** to their reports while figuring out how to undermine their peers. One of the Merriam-Webster dictionary's definitions of the word is "political activities characterized by artful and often dishonest practices."

I propose that we reconsider the word 'politics,' especially when used in a work context. The word, and the techniques ascribed to it, are inherently neither good nor bad. You can use politics for ill intent or good. Good intention aims for a win-win solution, whereas bad intent aims for a win-lose solution. Instead, let's use this different Merriam-Webster definition for the word "politics": "the total complex of relations between people living in society." For our purposes, let's call the company we work in our society. A company is a society in that it can have a panoply of personal relationships, group dynamics, shared goals, and systems of governance.

If we can get over our initial reaction to being political, how can we use some of these techniques for win-win solutions to problems?

Thinking politically means thinking ahead (being strategic), understanding the motivations of the people you need to convince (having empathy), and understanding the interactions of the systems you are trying to influence (systems thinking). You are working to make something happen—something you cannot do on your own. You may be working to overcome resistance to a new idea in a conservative institution. You could be trying to persuade another group to help your team with a project that will be good for the company but might make that group miss their quarterly goals.

Thinking politically will help you gain support for your ideas, soften resistance to change, and focus people on the bigger picture. If you improve everyone's situation, your peers will appreciate you, and you will find the way forward easier in the future. Conversely, done poorly, where you or your team move ahead at the expense of others, you will find it increasingly hard to gather support in the future.

PLAYING POLITICS SO EVERYBODY WINS: A PERSONAL EXAMPLE

In the early days of the public cloud, I worked in a company that already had established data centers worldwide. Getting a new server racked meant requisitioning a server from the central IT organization, following all their guidelines around the machine's configuration and which technologies could be used on it, and giving them access to maintain and manage it. The process to get a single server going with a public-facing interface could take months.

I was leading a new team trying to incubate an innovative product. We had adopted a Lean Startup[30] approach, moving to get to market in under six months. As this was a brand-new area for the company, we couldn't be sure how quickly the public would adopt the product, and we wanted the ability to add capacity quickly if needed or shut the project down if it wasn't getting traction. The company's lead time for servers was not going to work for us. So, we decided to leverage Amazon's young AWS offering. I knew that this would be a controversial decision and might incur opposition from other teams, especially IT. I could have chosen to "ask forgiveness, not permission" and hope that my small team could fly under the radar long enough to launch, but that was very risky. Our actions could be interpreted as a deliberate avoidance of company security and budget policies, which could prevent us from launching if we were found out.

I spoke to my peers in other teams to understand their prior experience working with the centralized IT team. I learned that if I approached the IT team directly for permission to use the public cloud, I would get an immediate "no." That would put me in a position of having to get their decision overruled, which would take a lot of time and energy. I decided to go a different route.

I put together a presentation on our plan for our product. I included our quick path to market to mitigate risk for the company, our plan to leverage the public cloud (to scale quickly and manage cost-effectively), and how we would address any corporate security concerns. The goal of the presentation was to build trust that my team was thinking about the business and not just playing with new technology, and to show that we had answers to the issues I expected other groups to raise. I portrayed our product plan as an innovative experiment in new product development—a low-risk approach to moving faster as a company. I wanted to get some protection for my team at a level that would short-circuit other teams worried about this new way of doing things.

After working with my boss to ensure I had their unequivocal support, we got time on my SVP's calendar to discuss the plan. I prepared for any argument against the plan, but I also left room for input from the SVP to help them feel invested so they would help protect the project. We left the meeting with approval for our approach and moved forward quickly enough to launch the product within our six-month window.

The product was more successful and grew more quickly than we had planned. Our public cloud adoption made it far easier for us to scale as the number of our customers did. Our success also increased our visibility within the company, however. The teams invested in managing and growing our worldwide data center infrastructure now started to see us as a threat. I began to have many increasingly tense meetings with them to discuss moving into the corporate infrastructure. I could have used my product's success to force the other team to back off, but that would have created even more enmity, setting up our teams for friction forever.

Instead of using my team's success as a wedge to ignore the IT team's demands, I worked with them to understand why we had to make the decision we had. I also identified what they could do to make switching to the internal infrastructure an easy decision for us and for other teams considering following in our footsteps. I committed my team to switching to the company's infrastructure as soon as it could support us.

Reading through that experience, you can see several political maneuvers I used to get my team the space we needed to ship our product.

- Talking to my peers to understand what their experiences and anticipate challenges. Consulting my peers on the problem got them enlisted as allies. If I were successful, they would have a better chance of success themselves in the future. **(systems thinking/having empathy)**
- Building a strategy to prevent the central IT organization from stopping my team's plan. **(being strategic)**
- Enlisting my manager meant I had an ally in my effort to convince other senior managers, someone who understood the SVP's motivations and concerns. **(having empathy)**
- Preparing my argument to the SVP not just to convince but also to engage. Making the executive not just an approver of the plan but a participant with a stake in its success. **(being strategic/systems thinking/having empathy)**

If I had stopped at this point or pressed my new advantage over the IT team, that would have been the type of corporate politics that people despise. I would have created a win-lose situation (and some very angry co-workers who would have justifiably felt I'd wronged them).

Instead, I took the following steps to help the group I felt I had to work around and improve the situation for everyone at the company:

- I used the lessons we learned from AWS to help the centralized IT team understand groups like ours with less predictable or forecastable needs. (having empathy/systems thinking)
- I committed to them that if they could support our needs (with our help), we would switch to the "official" infrastructure. (having empathy/being strategic)

Making sure we helped the IT team was more work for my team, but it was better for them and the company at large. It made the solution a win-win.

An outside observer, especially a jaded one, could look at each of my actions in a very different light. That observer would say that I schemed to isolate the IT team, skirted appropriate behavior, and cheated by going over their heads. If I hadn't then gone back to help lift the IT team, I might agree.

One might say that the best thing to do would have been to work with the centralized IT team to convince them that they should allow and support my plan. I would agree with that sentiment if it were possible to gain the IT team's support and ship my product on schedule. However, the experience of my peers told me otherwise. Those who have worked at large corporations with siloed functions working against different goals understand how intractable those other groups can be.

DON'T BE A PLAYER OF THE P-WORD

When faced with a challenge at work, try to understand the motivations of the people you work with and the systems they operate within. From there, build a strategy to achieve your goal. If you can achieve your goal while helping others move towards theirs in the long term, you will be an innovator and a team player within the society that is your company. On the other hand, if you achieve your goal at the expense of others, you will be nothing more than a player of the unspeakable p-word.

CHAPTER 13

Protecting your team from layoffs

Originally published on October 3, 2014

It's that time of year again; when my inbox and social media feeds fill with news of former coworkers who got caught in my old company's yearly layoff exercise.

I'd like to say that I was lucky that in eight years as a manager there I didn't have to lay off anyone, but it was a lot of very hard work. So, for my former colleagues or any manager, here are some tips to help you keep your team visible and vital in a large company. It was never a matter of just the groups or individuals doing a poor job would get hit. It was the teams and individuals who weren't visible beyond their immediate peers. If management doesn't know who you are or why what you do is important, they are far less likely to keep you around.

STAY FOCUSED ON COMPANY PRIORITIES

Senior management hopefully is making the company priorities clear. Unfortunately, an anti-pattern I often have seen is to ignore these messages because "It will just shift again. I'm working on the critical stuff." This attitude is willfully ignoring that clear prioritization message. It is equivalent to saying that you are smarter than your company's senior leadership. This may be true, but I guarantee they have much more insight into the competitive landscape than you do. Ignoring them is not only lousy self-preservation, but it is also disrespectful.

As a leader, you must always ensure that your team works on items relevant to the company's priorities. This doesn't mean you should completely pivot every time priorities change, but you should adapt your team's mission to support those priorities.

KEEP YOUR TEAM AND TEAM MEMBERS VISIBLE

It has been said that the best way to promote yourself as a manager is to hire people more intelligent than you and support them as best as you can. This is true in my experience.

If you have smart people, ensure they are visible in the larger organization. Give them public kudos for work well done and opportunities to demonstrate their brilliance, like internal tech talks or blog posts.

The visibility of bright individuals has a halo effect on their team, especially if there are multiple bright folks on the team. At layoff time, your team will be too awesome to mess with. Building a bright team also reflects well on you as their manager.

I want to make one thing clear, however. Visibility isn't about people tooting their own horn over mediocre accomplishments. It is about doing good work and then talking about it. *Intelligence without application is valueless.* Do something extraordinary aligned with company goals, and then talk about it. Share the knowledge and share the lessons with others. I call this "taking a victory lap."

MANAGE OUT LOW PERFORMERS

This advice may seem counter-intuitive in a layoff-prone company. For example, you might think you should keep your low performers around if you may some day need to lay someone off. But unfortunately, this is incorrect on multiple levels.

First, it is a jerk move. If you have folks struggling in your environment/culture, you aren't doing them any favors by keeping them around as "cannon fodder." If they are a bad fit and haven't improved with all manner of coaching and mentoring, help them find a better role. It is the best thing you can do for them.

Second, they bring the rest of their team down. The rest of your team may be great, but those low performers will be a drag on the whole team, performance and morale-wise.

Poor performers give you and your team a negative vibe, just like high-performing folks give you a positive one. When it comes time for senior management to cut people, having known poor performers makes you a target. Instead, build a reputation for raising the level of your worst performers or managing out the ones you can't help. Actively managing your team will help inoculate your employees from a layoff. When senior management decides to lay off, it may not just be your lowest performers that are affected. Better to protect the whole team and do the right thing for people who would be happier elsewhere.

MANAGE UP

This guidance may sound political or calculating, but it isn't meant that way. When I say, "manage up," I mean actively communicating with your manager and soliciting help or feedback when needed.

Your manager is busy. They are probably unaware of what is happening in every team in their organization. If you have great performers in your team, tell your boss when they accomplish something noteworthy. If you have folks with issues, let your boss know what you are doing to help them. Let your boss know how you align your team's goals with the company and its goals. Then get feedback. What could you be doing better? Is there something you are missing strategically? By nature of their place in the organization, they have more visibility into what is happening across the company. Take advantage of that.

Knowing more about your team and its capabilities will be necessary when a senior leader looks across their organization to decide where to make some tough cuts.

THESE TECHNIQUES AREN'T JUST FOR PROTECTING THE TEAM FROM LAYOFFS

Hopefully, these tips shouldn't seem only like good ways to manage against layoffs but like good strategies for managing, period. You should always recognize top performers for their work, raise the level or manage out the low performers, align with the company's priorities, and make sure your boss knows what is going on.

CHAPTER 14

Every decision creates a policy

Originally published on July 26, 2021

It seems like a simple question. "Can I expense these headphones?" or "Can we write this service in Elixir?"

The person asking may have a good reason. They may have an excellent performance history. The request is simple; why not grant it? You are an experienced manager, the proposal seems reasonable, and you want your team to like you.

We may make dozens of small decisions each week without considering their implications. These decisions, however, unintentionally create policies for our team or our organization that we will have to contend with later.

A simple expense decision for a single team member often doesn't make sense when applied to everyone on the team. Your rationale for granting the first request rings hollow when denying it to someone else. You may or may not realize that your decision violates a company policy or has unintended consequences for the finance or legal teams. When challenged by these teams, you are forced to rescind your decision, thus disappointing your team member and suggesting that you aren't empowered to make these decisions.

Allowing a developer to use a new language to write a service may let them grow their technical skills. It quickly becomes problematic when other developers on the team want to use different languages, and your codebase becomes increasingly challenging to maintain.

Each request you grant or deny is inevitably shared with everyone on your team and with other teams as well. When it is shared, the details and reasoning behind the original decision are often lost. When a second person comes forward with what they think is a similar request and you respond differently, it suggests that you act capriciously or play favorites. When a person on another team asks the same from their lead, using your decision as justification, you put that manager in an awkward position.

Some companies give a lot of autonomy to their leads. This freedom helps teams to move faster and gives them more ownership and accountability. However, suppose the leaders in these teams make inconsistent decisions about travel, benefits, job offers, promotions, or software architecture. The result is eventually chaos. To the company employees, it seems that the leadership is uncoordinated and full of conflict. Lacking any clear reasoning on why different teams do things differently, people will try to invent rationales, which are usually wrong and can sometimes assume the worst in management.

As inconsistent leadership produces increasingly low morale, the result is often an overcorrection: senior company leadership creates new, excessively rigid policies to clear the accumulated management debt. This correction can often feel like "the hammer coming down" or a startup suddenly feeling "very corporate."

Even if the problems and corrections aren't so extreme, these simple, beneficial actions will help you to be more consistent with your peers.

WHEN THERE IS A NEW SITUATION

If someone on the team approaches you with a novel request, do not give them an immediate, definitive answer. Instead, let the person know that you will investigate and get back to them. If you have established company policies for expensing, remote working, software architecture, or something else that may cover the situation, check there first.

If the answer is not definitive, raise your intended response to your manager. If it is about benefits or expensing, include the most appropriate HR representative. This step may seem unnecessary at first, but if you are clear that you are trying to be consistent with others, that should help your team member to understand.

WHEN YOU WANT AN EXCEPTION TO AN EXISTING POLICY

If the issue isn't new, but you think the situation warrants an exception to the policy, you need to think carefully. The exception may be wholly justified, but will this invite more people to seek exceptions? How can you clearly and objectively state the reasons for granting this exception? How will you update the policy to carve out this specific exception? While it can be uncomfortable not to give an exception to someone you think deserves it, it may be the right decision in the long run.

If you wish to create an exception to an existing policy, let the person know that you'll need to discuss it with management due to the current guidelines. Document your reasoning for the exception and share it with your manager and, if relevant, someone from the people team or HR department. You'll need their support and approval.

DOCUMENT THE DECISION

If you decide on a new policy or are changing an existing policy, it is good practice to document the decision and share it with your peers. A simple one-page document describing the situation; the thought process on the resolution; the existing company policies or other peer decisions that influenced this choice; the decision itself; any caveats around the decision; and the outcome for the individual affected.

Share this document with your peers. You may choose to get their input before finalizing the decision since it will affect them as well. Again, you are creating a precedent.

If you are looking for a specific template, there are the Toyota A3[31], or the Spotify DIBB[32]. For software architecture, the Architecture Decision Record[33] are documents that many organizations use.

Suppose you are part of a particularly transparent organization. In this case, you may want to share a redacted version (to protect the individual's privacy) with the rest of the organization. Over time these decisions can be collected and refined into a new handbook for your organization.

ISN'T THIS OVERLY COMPLICATED?

This suggested process may seem more complicated than it needs to be. "To make a simple decision about expensing headphones, I need to consult the employee handbook, ask my manager and HR, write up a one-page decision document and then send it to my peers?" It does seem like a lot of work.

Consider the alternative.

In a one-on-one, someone from your team asks if they can take a vacation for two weeks right before the team's big deadline. When you say that the timing is not suitable for the team, they tell you about their friend on another team who was allowed to do precisely that. Talking to the other lead, they say that they didn't think it was a problem. Do you now become the mean manager that doesn't let people on the team take a vacation, or do you put the team's commitment in jeopardy to be consistent with your peers?

This scenario may seem far-fetched, but it happens all the time. Especially in scaling organizations that move from being a relatively unconstrained startup to a more structured company. The best thing for everybody on the team is for managers to be consistent, and to be consistent, they must communicate.

For your organization, you may find more straightforward ways to communicate decisions and achieve consistency between leads. If so, please share them!

CHAPTER 15

What do I look for when hiring an engineer?

Originally published on November 2, 2013

I don't spend much time on Quora, but I came across the question: "What qualities should a software engineer have?[34]" Anyone who has worked with me can tell you that I am pretty opinionated about this subject. So since someone wasn't already saying what I would have, I decided to post an answer. Here is that answer:

Over the last couple of decades, I've interviewed hundreds of software engineers for my teams at Microsoft, Adobe, Spotify, and other places.

Over the years, I've honed in on a few things that I consider vital for anyone joining my organization. These are the kinds of things that I value as a hiring manager, of course. Others will have their critical criteria.

These are in rough priority order.

1. **Pragmatism** I don't bother with tricky or difficult programming questions designed to test a corner of your knowledge or some trivia. Instead, I ask a dead simple question—something anyone could do. Then I complicate it. And complicate it again. And again. I look for the point where you can no longer adapt your first answer. I want to know that you will throw away your first answer when it no longer makes sense. You'd be amazed how many engineers will hack on something that will never work when they could throw it away and do something much more straightforward in a quarter of the time.

2. **Interest** Do you actually like writing code every day? Do you read programming blogs for fun? Do you work on your own coding projects outside of work? If this will be your job, I want someone overjoyed that they get paid to write software, not someone who'd rather be doing something else.

3. **Attitude/humility** I've worked with brilliant people who are jerks. For every inch they moved the product forward with their innovation or genius, they moved the project back two inches by being impossible to work with. I want someone who will improve the team, not someone who feels everyone "needs to do as they are told." (Yes, an actual quote from a candidate.)

4. **Intelligence** Yeah, you do need to be smart. Writing software is part art and requires creativity, but it is also a lot about problem-solving and just sheer brainpower to figure out why this thing is crashing, but only on Tuesday when the moon is full.

5. **Programming languages/domain experience** I have worked professionally with a dozen or more programming languages. Some I don't even remember anymore. While I have a lot of depth in some of them through years of experience, I have learned others as I need to in order to suit the project. I would prefer to see someone proficient in more than one language because that shows some breadth and a willingness to learn, but if you can code and are clever (see #4), you can probably pick up whatever language we are working in reasonably fast. I hire for the long term. If you're a good fit, we can take a bit longer to get you up to speed, similarly with domain experience. If you have an aptitude, we can teach you.

I do have a couple of caveats to #5, though: If I'm hiring for a senior position that requires domain knowledge, yeah, that is in the job requirements, so you need to bring that. However, you would still need to handle 1-4, in any case.

On languages, there is a significant caveat. If we're doing C++ or C, you'll need some experience there. If you've only ever worked with high-level, garbage-collected languages, bringing you up to speed will take too long. I've tried this too many times and realized that it usually isn't worth the effort.

CHAPTER 16

A resignation can be an opportunity

Originally published on August 27, 2020

People leave jobs. If you are a manager, people will leave your team, just as someday you will leave your team.

When this happens it is an opportunity, a chance to re-evaluate. While you might want to immediately pull out the job description that you used when hiring for the role last time, instead, take some time to think.

A CHANCE TO LEARN

When someone tells you that they are resigning, it can feel personal: 'they don't like working for me.' It can hurt. You might immediately look for any reason why it isn't your fault. It is natural to want to move on as quickly as possible. You may even obsess about everything that you could have done differently.

Instead, after an employee gives you notice, take a day or two to process and get some distance. Recenter. Then meet with them. Come back to them with an open mind. Do not look to assign blame, let them know that you are working to improve the team for the people that are still here. Ask what did not work for them and what they will miss, aiming not to assign any extra meaning to what they say. Take notes. Thank them.

Take some more time to create mental distance, then come back again and think about the leaver's words. Try to understand from their perspective what they experienced. If they are taking a more senior role elsewhere, was there a similar opportunity in your company that you could have helped them get? If they are joining another company to learn a different technology, was it a technology they could have explored in your organization? Was there another team in your company that they could have joined instead?

Your goal is to understand their unmet needs. Were there signs that you missed? Were there opportunities in your company or in your team that could have addressed their needs?

Once again, the goal is not to assign blame, and the goal is not to get the employee to change their mind either. The goal is to learn from this experience.

So moving forward, how can you approach your role in a better way?

Consider this process to be a personal retrospective, and just like in an Agile team retrospective, you may want to emerge with a list of things to keep doing, a list of things to start doing, and a list of things to stop doing.

A CHANCE TO CHANGE

As teams evolve they shift and mature. If the leaver has been in the group for a long time, they may have accumulated an unusual set of responsibilities and they may have influenced the technical decisions around their strengths.

While it may seem like the obvious decision is to look for someone with the same skill set, that is just 'role inertia' (credit to Omosola Odetunde[35] for introducing that phrase to me). Instead think of this as an opportunity to re-evaluate and make a change without impacting someone.

Consider your technical vision for the team and the skill sets of others in the group. Is there something missing that could help you today or in the future? Is this role still needed? Should you repurpose the position into a different one based on the team's long-term needs?

It is critical to think about long-term needs and not short-term ones. A mistake managers often make is that they hire someone because of near-term demand. They assume that there will be a headcount later to cover the long-term need, but too often that headcount doesn't appear and now the team is missing a crucial skill set.

Potentially your team is out of balance, where you have too many (or too few) senior folks. This opportunity means you can now rebalance the levels within the group. Maybe this role is no longer necessary and you can give a headcount to another team that needs it more, or potentially there is someone on the team who is looking for a new challenge and can step into the role.

If you are in a position where you manage multiple teams then this may be an opportunity to re-evaluate the team structure, especially if the leaver is a manager. A way to approach this exercise would be to imagine that the person leaving was never on the team. Your manager has given you a brand new headcount and asked you to figure out how you want to use it.

Once you have a plan, you can then write the job description and look to fill the role, as you may decide that you need to replace the person with someone who has a similar skill set. If so, you can move forward confidently knowing that you have thought it through, and if you have also taken the time to learn you will hopefully retain your new hire for a long time.

CHAPTER 17

Addressing the challenges of partially distributed engineering teams

Originally published on May 17, 2021

As companies begin planning their approach to post-pandemic life, patterns are starting to emerge.

Some companies are planning to return to their offices and carry on as they did before. Others are adopting a partially distributed structure, reopening some of their offices but not assigning desks or requiring employees to work there. Some companies have even switched to being fully distributed.

In a fully co-located team, every member is in the same office near each other, nearly every day. A fully distributed team has every member in a different physical location almost every day. Everything else is partially co-located/partially distributed/ Hybrid. Even if you all work in the same physical office, if people are there on different days, you are only partially co-located.

The tech industry has consistently demonstrated creativity and innovation in how work is structured. Companies like Automattic, GitLab, and others have long shared lessons on how fully distributed teams can be effective; decades of business books have addressed the challenges of leadership in co-located teams, but there isn't as much published wisdom on leading partially distributed teams beyond the suggestion of treating them as fully distributed.

I have led fully co-located teams, fully distributed teams, and partially distributed teams. I have always said that the partially distributed is the hardest to do well.

THE PROBLEMS WITH BEING PARTIALLY DISTRIBUTED

Inconsistent communication speeds

The most significant problem with being partially co-located is that you quickly fall into asymmetric communication patterns. Folks in the same physical locations have very high bandwidth conversations, but everyone else communicates at a fraction of the efficiency.

The bandwidth issue extends beyond group meetings where some are in a conference room and others are on video, and permeates spontaneous meetings, too: people talking at the coffee machine, at lunch, or bumping into each other in the hall. People are more inclined to call out to a colleague they can physically see rather than trying to reach one over chat or video.

These spontaneous conversations might inspire solutions to team challenges that don't involve the larger group, creating friction. The team can splinter as the people who follow similar schedules end up working together more frequently. Distrust builds within the team, especially if some are in other cities or have other commitments preventing them from being present when their peers are. Parts of the group may feel isolated or left out of the decision-making process.

This inconsistent communication bandwidth can significantly impact the design of the team's deliverables due to the effects of Conway's Law[36]: 'Any organization that designs a system (defined broadly) will produce a design whose structure is a copy of the organization's communication structure.'

Unequal visibility of work

People naturally have a recency bias, tending to prefer recent events over historical ones. They also have more of a personal connection with those they interact with in person over those on a video call (a familiarity bias). Both biases work against those who are physically present less often. The lack of direct visibility of you or your team relative to other groups can be a significant disadvantage for you, the team, or individuals when it is time for performance reviews or recognition. Even if the team members have worked hard to achieve a goal, if they were not literally visible and other individuals were, you will have to overcome those biases to justify raises or promotions.

Inconsistent working hours

If your team is spread over many time zones, you get the classic problem of people having to wait on others when they need assistance, clarification, or to hand-off work. This problem can also happen with teams in near time zones if part of the team works from home to better incorporate their outside-of-work responsibilities or have a more flexible schedule. Unless addressed through restructuring the way work flows or introducing other constraints, work stalls in the team and people get frustrated.

ADDRESSING THE CHALLENGES

Create consistent expectations of availability

If most of the team plans to work two or three days in the office each week, have the team agree on which days that will be. So that when the group is in the office, most of the people are there.

If people need to accommodate their time zone or outside-of-work commitments, mutually agree on shared working hours. During those times, people are expected to be online and available for discussions or questions. Those hours do not need to be contiguous!

Ensure that people on the team are proactively communicating their availability so that others know when they can reach out or expect faster responses. It may be helpful to have a shared team calendar where every member puts their expected working hours for the week and adjusts that calendar if something comes up.

If possible, avoid being partially distributed

If nearly everyone on your team plans to return to the office, it might make sense for the people who plan to work off-site to switch to a mainly distributed team and vice-versa. It may seem extreme to suggest that people switch to another group, but it will make things easier for them and for their teams to be fully distributed or fully co-located.

Make sure that your team is visible

The adage, 'out of sight, out of mind' speaks to a truth about human nature. Suppose your organization's leadership is working from the office, and you or members of your team are primarily working from other locations. In that case, it is vital to make sure that the individuals' and teams' work is visible.

Invite your manager to your virtual team demos or ask them to stop by your team meeting or standup. Proactively tell your boss when individuals exceed your expectations. Invite your manager to set up occasional skip-level meetings with the distributed people in the group. If your boss has office hours, encourage members of your team to attend from time to time. These strategies to increase visibility are helpful even for entirely co-located organizations, but they are crucial for partially distributed teams.

Take opportunities to build empathy

Video meetings can become very transactional, especially when it seems like the workday is full of them. Without the spontaneous conversations and connections that arise from chance meetings in an office, you can start to forget that the people on your team are actual humans and not just pixels on a screen. Take time in your meetings for small talk, and don't feel like you have to force people immediately back to the agenda if the team digresses into talking about their favorite TV shows or places they want to visit. These human details remind everyone that their co-workers are people with lives and motivations. It encourages empathy.

When the whole team can travel safely and without concern, bring them together on a regular cadence (the frequency determined by the travel budget and people's freedom to travel). Spending time with each other will encourage much more profound empathy between the people on the team.

Move communication offline as much as possible

Co-located teams avoid many meetings by stopping by each other's desks for a five-minute chat. When you can't see the person, a very natural thing to do is to book a 30-minute meeting for that conversation instead and invite several others who might have input while you are at it, thus guaranteeing that it will use all 30 minutes (and may run over).

Fully distributed teams have long favored written communication as the primary tool to document decision-making and be more inclusive of colleagues spread across time zones. This model was also pioneered and perfected by large open-source projects where wide geographic distribution is the norm.

Enforcing an offline-first communication and decision-making process within your team helps ameliorate the challenges of non-overlapping work schedules and brings increased symmetry to communication speeds.

Take a remote-first approach to team meetings

As I mentioned above, a common suggestion for partially co-located teams is to have everyone dial into group meetings even if they are sitting near each other; treating all as if they are distributed helps put everyone on an equal footing in the discussion. Still, it is not always possible if there are no adequate facilities in the office to support that. Alternatives would be to have whoever leads the meeting always dial in from another location or have the bulk of team meetings on days the group has decided to work from home.

WE'RE NOT DONE CHANGING; THIS IS AN OPPORTUNITY!

Just over a year ago, most companies were comfortable with their ways of working or were evolving them slowly – but the pandemic forced all companies to adjust to new ways of operating immediately. Finding a 'new normal' will be a much more gradual process, with much uncertainty.

As an engineering leader, there is a massive opportunity to find new ways for your team to be effective in this new world of work. You and the group should approach the challenge with flexibility and a willingness to experiment.

Share the ideas you learn with your peers and the larger organization. If companies struggle to make this new flexibility in work successful, they will quickly move back to their old ways of doing things.

You can help your company be a leader in providing flexibility and freedom to its employees while also being effective at delivering value to your customers. When you figure things out, please share them with the rest of us; we're on this 'new normal' journey together.

CHAPTER 18

Twenty questions for your 1:1s

Originally published on May 17, 2021

You sit down for a chat with someone on your team. You get through the pleasantries, the small talk, the status, and you run out of things to say. It happens to even the most curious and high-EQ people. It happens to me, and I have probably had 10,000 one-on-one meetings in my career.

When you hit that moment where neither of you has anything to say, it is very tempting just to say, "Ok then! Let's talk next week." giving you both time back into your day. If this happens occasionally, it is not a severe problem. However, if you find it happening more often than you would like, it is good to keep some prompts handy to move into deeper topics that might prompt a valuable conversation.

Here are twenty questions that you might find helpful if you get stuck at the surface level or run out of things to discuss in your one-on-ones:

1. What is more challenging in your day-to-day work than it should be?
2. What is the most fulfilling thing that has happened this week?
3. Who on the team has impressed you lately?
4. What are you looking forward to in the next six months? Why?
5. What haven't you told me that I probably should know?
6. What is one thing that you miss from your last job/team?
7. Who on the team are you most worried about?
8. If there is one thing I could change about your role today, what would it be?
9. Who on another team do you most enjoy working with?
10. What do you wonder about?
11. How would you change the company's strategy?
12. What is the product or feature that we should build next?
13. When do you feel the most satisfied at work?
14. What is your least favorite part of your job?
15. What percentage of your work time do you think you are in a flow state?
16. What is the one meeting that you would add to your calendar?
17. What is the one meeting that you would remove from your calendar?
18. What do you wish that I did differently?

19. What should I keep doing?
20. When am I the most helpful?

If you don't like any of these questions, you can create your own list in a few minutes. You are looking for a question that gets the other person to think, share a bit more with you, and hopefully give you an avenue for deeper discussion.

CHAPTER 19

Writing Useful Performance Reviews: Assembling the data

Originally published on December 4, 2021

It's December, and that can mean only one thing. For many of us, it is now—or soon will be—time to write performance reviews for our team. Writing reviews can be daunting for many, especially those with large groups or little experience. I often hear managers (even senior leaders) bemoaning the effort it takes to write the reviews for their group members. However, there are some things you can do that will make the process less onerous, no matter what format or schedule your company has.

WHY DO WE DO PERFORMANCE REVIEWS?

The rationale we used to hear for performance reviews is that they are for the employee to know how they are doing, to give them helpful feedback on what they are doing well and where they need to improve. Today we try to provide this feedback often, throughout the year. I often tell the managers on my teams that there shouldn't be any surprises in the performance review. It should instead be a summing up of the feedback that the person has been receiving all along.

If we give feedback throughout the review period, why do we need to do the performance review? It is for the company and us almost as much as it is for the person receiving it. Ideally, we maintain a narrative across the year with our feedback, reviewing months of our notes and prior communication before each one-on-one. All too often, the larger arc gets lost in the whirlwind of work. The feedback we give is usually very transactional about what has just occurred. If there are significant overarching discussions, we may be able to tie the feedback to that, but often the narrative gets lost.

The review is a chance to look across all that has transpired over a much lengthier period than the time between one-on-ones. It is a chance for us to take stock and find new patterns or trends that we may have missed. To look at the bigger picture and then build a shared understanding of that picture with the team member.

The review is also for the company because the company keeps a record of employee performance to justify bonuses, promotions, salary increases, and stock offerings. It is also vital to have a history of performance for a new manager if you move on from your role. Sometimes you will move to a new job, or the employee will move to a new team. When that happens, all the shared understanding you have built up is lost unless it's written down. An employee who has been working years towards a new role may be set back significantly if their new manager doesn't understand the efforts they have made over time and is looking only at what they see in the present moment.

A well-written review is a valuable document for the person receiving it. First, it is a checkpoint for them to refer to as they work towards their career goals. Second, it is a useful document for you to help them on their career path. Third, it is a favor to their future managers at your company. Finally, it is a critical document for the company and your manager to understand how to manage compensation for the person.

PREPARING FOR THE PERFORMANCE REVIEW. START EARLY!

Often writing reviews seems like a great deal of work because we wait until our company's official "kick-off" of the review period. The people/HR team lets all the managers know the schedule, does a few meetings to discuss/update the process, and opens the forms for managers to enter data. If you wait for that moment to begin preparing your reviews, you may find yourself spending a lot of nights and weekends trying to get your evaluations prepared, since your regular work continues during this time. In the past, I've spent more than a few sad weekend days sitting in a ski lodge huddled over my laptop, writing reviews while my family was out on the slopes having fun.

Reviews happen at the same time every year.

Your company may adjust the dates slightly, but you can be confident that reviews will happen around the same time each year. When the dates are announced, you should be prepared. If you are incredibly diligent, you may be collecting and organizing data for your reviews year-round. If you haven't done that, you can start reviewing, amassing, and organizing supporting data as review time approaches so that you don't have to struggle and potentially miss things. While the format of the reviews in your company may change periodically, the general things that are measured likely won't.

THERE ARE MANY SOURCES OF DATA YOU CAN ASSEMBLE FOR THE REVIEW.

As I start my preparation, I create a folder on my computer for the review period and a subfolder for each person. In each folder, I assemble all the documents and data for the performance assessment. I prefer to keep local copies because it is less likely that I will accidentally share the folder or file. To focus, I often go offsite to work on reviews, and sometimes these places have sketchy connectivity. Having the documents stored on my laptop has functioned well for my process.

My primary data always comes from the notes I take during my one-on-ones and in meetings.

I used to store all my notes in Evernote organized by meeting (for recurring meetings) and tagged with the people in the discussion. This storage approach made it easy to find all my notes for each person to track what we spoke about across the review period. However, during the pandemic, I switched to paper notebooks. Now I keep an index of which pages people appear on. This index makes it easy to find all my notes referencing someone.

As I review my meeting notes, I assemble meaningful comments or things I notice into a new document in the person's folder to organize my data for the review. I include where I got it from for each item in case I need to go back to the source.

The person's prior reviews are essential.

I always download copies of any previous reviews for the person in the system and put them in the folder. It is vital to remember our prior review conversations and see any reviews from before they reported to me. Reading previous reviews helps me understand the different challenges and strengths they have had and understand their career story at the company so far.

E-mail and Slack exchanges may remind you of other events from the year.

Occasionally, things come up and are resolved between one-on-ones or meetings, so they don't appear in your notes. I scan over the e-mail and Slack exchanges I have had with the person during the review period to see if I missed an event in reviewing my meeting notes.

I copy/paste these exchanges into the notes document in the person's review folder, or summarize them there.

Make a list of peers of the person from whom you want to request feedback.

Your company may include a formal peer-review element in your performance reviews process. However, if it isn't part of the company process, you will still find it valuable to ask for peer review feedback. The first step is to list the people you would like to ask for feedback, so you are ready. You may also write the template for the peer feedback request to prepare you to send them out.

I've noticed that in companies with a formal peer feedback process as part of their reviews, people quickly become inundated with feedback requests. Your chance of getting valuable (or any) feedback is greatly improved if you send the request early, before people have feedback fatigue.

If you know that peer feedback will not be part of your company's process, you may still want to send out the feedback requests early to get the responses with enough time to follow up if there are questions. However, make sure that you specify a date by which you would like the feedback returned, and don't make that date too far in the future, or people will put the request aside and forget about it.

The message template goes into the top-level performance reviews folder, and the list goes into the person's folder. If you want to be tricky, you can put the list in a CSV file to make it easier for a mail merge. You may generate a lot of e-mail performance feedback requests as part of this process. I've automated this over the years.

When you receive the feedback, save a copy of it to the folder.

You may need to ask for a self-evaluation.

If your company does not include self-evaluation as part of the review process, you may ask the people you review to do that for you. If you are unsure what to ask, use your company's career pathing rubric for their job/level. Ask them to compare themselves to the rubric and give examples of how they have met, exceeded, or missed the expectations. If you use individual goals or OKRs[37], they should talk about how they achieved or missed them. They should also talk about the areas they want to improve on for the coming review period.

You want them to complete their self-review early enough that you have time to follow up with them or others on anything that comes up in that document. Your company will set the dates for you if it includes self-review as part of the review process.

Save the self-evaluation to the person's folder.

Review the work output.

A critical part of the performance review is reviewing the actual value the person created for the customers and company. A portion of your performance review as a lead or manager covers what your team achieved. Think through your teams' accomplishments and think about how this person contributed to or detracted from those projects. Add concrete examples to the notes document.

Look over the person's commits to the code of the project. Did they review others' code? Did they contribute helpful comments? Did their code require many fixes? Did they contribute to the project documentation? Look over their comments in your project and bug tracking systems. Did they contribute helpful information? Did they help others?

It can be very tempting to try to be "objective" when looking at work output. Counting lines of code produced, number of commits, number of issues filed or closed, or story points completed might seem like unbiased data. Avoid this temptation at all costs. People have different approaches to knowledge work. Even if your team has strong guidelines on how work should be done, people will always have methods that your seemingly objective process might miss. Instead, focus on the value they contribute to the team and watch in the peer feedback for what they contribute that won't show up in the source management or issue tracking systems.

Save your observations on their work output in your notes document.

WHAT IF THE PERSON DIDN'T REPORT TO ME FOR THE ENTIRE REVIEW PERIOD?

If the person is a new hire and is still eligible for a performance review, you will use this process, but just for their time in the company. You will have to make allowances for their onboarding and focus more on how they learn to contribute than on their actual contributions.

If you are a new manager to an existing team, spend as much time as you can with the prior manager to understand how they have approached each person's development. Read the reviews for each person before talking to the manager. If the manager has left the company, you can still reach out to them. Hopefully, they will still want the best for their old team. Depending on how long you were in the team during the review period, you may need to emphasize the peer review component more than you would have otherwise. Be aware that changing a team's manager is very disruptive to the team. You will only have seen the results of that disruption and how the team now works.

If the person joined the team from a different group in the company, consider doing a joint review with their prior manager to cover their work before joining your team. If that doesn't seem necessary, you should still have an extended conversation with their former manager after going over the person's previous reviews.

THIS PROCESS SEEMS LIKE A LOT OF WORK!

It is! It should be. It is important stuff. Think about the best reviews you have received from your current or former managers. Not just the performance reviews that were the most positive, but the ones that made you feel like your manager cared about your development. A good review inspires you with the knowledge that your manager and the company recognize the worthy work you've done. You know that your areas of improvement have been considered and are essential for your career development.

A good review requires good data. Therefore, it is incumbent on you to make sure you are going over as much as you can, not just what you can remember at the end of the review period (also known as recency bias[38]).

The first time you go through this process, it will take a great deal of effort, but the payoff will be worth it. For the next period, you will learn to collect and organize this data as you go. If you assemble and categorize data all the time, it will be helpful in your one-to-ones as well and not just at performance review time.

NOW YOU HAVE THE DATA. WHAT NEXT?

Now that you have assembled your data, you can evaluate the data against the expectations of the role and level. I will discuss that in the next chapter.

CHAPTER 20

Writing Useful Performance Reviews: Evaluating the data and writing the review

Originally published on December 11, 2021

Once you have assembled your data, you are ready to write the review.

HAVE EVERYTHING READY BEFORE YOU BEGIN WRITING.

Before you begin to write your review, make sure you have the role and level definition for the person's current role and level. You should also have the description for the job at the next level. If you followed my suggestions in the previous chapter, you have the folder with earlier reviews, notes from 1:1s and project meetings, the peer feedback, the person's self-evaluation, and your notes on the work output. Your company's performance review form and supporting process documentation are necessary as well.

REVIEW YOUR DOCUMENTATION.

If you followed my advice from the last chapter, you have assembled a large amount of data. You will now go through it all to evaluate the person's performance relative to the standard. You may find it beneficial to highlight essential information in the documents as you review them or copy/paste them into a new file for easy reference.

If you can, do your review in one sitting. This process helps you build an understanding of the person's performance. You are creating a context with as much data as possible, so keeping it in your near-term memory is beneficial. If you don't have enough time to do this in one sitting or think you may be interrupted, take good notes that you can review after a break.

As you read over the data, you should be consciously building a narrative of the review period. Each person will have some highs and lows, but patterns of performance should emerge.

After reviewing the data, you should have one or two specific messages to convey to the person about their performance. That is the goal of data accumulation and evaluation.

Start with the review form.

First, read through the review form, making sure you understand the expectation for each question. Then, if you are in doubt, use the company documentation on the process. Get clarifications from your HR partner if necessary.

Understand the role/level definitions.

Make sure you understand the person's role expectations at the current level and the next level. The current level documentation covers the performance expectations the person should meet now. The next-level documentation is helpful for you to recognize performance beyond expectations.

Go over any previous reviews.

Read all the previous reviews the person has received at the company in chronological order. This review will help you see patterns and trends, and goals met and missed. The essential evaluations are the most recent, especially any from the last couple of years. Take extra care reading these to remind yourself of prior performance discussions (if you wrote them) and understand the current development areas.

What if you disagree with the assessments in reviews written by their previous manager?

Suppose the person is new to your team, or you are a new lead for an existing group. In that case, occasionally, you will read prior reviews and realize that the previous manager used a very different approach to performance than your own. Ideally, everyone is evaluating against the company's career pathing rubric, but sometimes it is applied differently. In this case, you may need to prepare for some challenging conversations.

You might choose to treat this review cycle as a transitional one, giving people time to adjust to your management style. If you do that, make sure they understand how future reviews will work differently.

Read through your notes from your review of e-mail or messaging exchanges.

Scanning through your messages from the review period will help remind you of any events, successes, or challenges that you may have forgotten about during the review period.

Study the work output to understand the person's contributions to their projects.

A reminder from the previous chapter: a person's code contributions do not reflect the sum of their contributions. Senior developers may contribute less code because they are more efficient or spend time helping other people. Look at code reviews, bug notes, documentation, Architectural Decision Records, or anything else that will demonstrate contributions to the team's projects.

You're probably arriving at some opinions at this point.

By this point, you will have started to build the narrative, identified some possible key discussion topics, and formed opinions on the person's performance. You likely started the process with ideas already, based on your interactions with the person over the review period. The views you bring at the start of the process aren't necessarily incorrect. Still, they may be untrustworthy because of recency bias[39] (giving more weight to recent events), affinity bias[40] (a tendency to prefer people similar to us or someone we know), or the person being very good at promoting their accomplishments (or taking credit for others' work).

Now you will start to review the more subjective data. Does what you find conflict with or reinforce your existing viewpoint?

Review the peer evaluations.

Peer evaluations can be problematic. First, they can be tempting to cheat for people by giving the chance to collude with their peers. Second, many people don't want to criticize their co-workers. Third, they may worry about how their comments reflect on themselves. For these reasons, you will want to read between the lines when reading peer evaluations.

As you read through the peer comments, look for examples that support or challenge the narrative you have been building.

If you find many things that challenge your message, you may reevaluate your opinions.

Read the self-evaluation last.

When people are evaluated based on something they produce, they naturally tend to create a narrative that accentuates their positive contributions and minimizes their negative ones. It isn't necessarily deceptive; it is human nature. Therefore, I always read the self-evaluation last. I don't want it to influence how I evaluate all the other data. However, the self-evaluation is still relevant because it is the person's view of how things have gone—their side of the story.

There are a few things I always look for when reading this document: Are there good explanations for some challenges they had during the review period? How aware are they of their challenges and strengths? Are there any comments that might be relevant for the reviews of others on the team? Where are they interested in growing? Finally, is there anything that you can do to support them better in the following review period?

Now, write the review!

Having reviewed all the data, you are now ready to write the review. You have one or two messages for your narrative as well as the data to support it.

Be clear.

One of the biggest mistakes people make when writing a review is trying not to be too negative or too positive. Particularly problematic is using the "compliment sandwich[41]" (surrounding a criticism with compliments) or vague language to avoid a challenging conversation when delivering the evaluation. Another mistake is creating a "balanced" review by overemphasizing small challenges or successes to offset a too positive or negative narrative.

When someone reads your review, they want to know if they are doing well or not doing well. If the person doesn't know after reading the evaluation, it is not helpful to them. In addition, they should have a clear connection between their review and their salary adjustment.

They can't all be extraordinary.

Often, I see inexperienced or poorly trained managers produce reviews for their teams that are uniformly good. "Everyone on the team is doing great!" they say. However, even on the highest-performing teams, some members will contribute more than others during a review period.

Universally positive reviews are a signal that a manager is either not promoting team members (so they are all overperforming relative to their level), not paying attention (they are missing things), not challenging the individuals on the team, or setting their expectations too low. Exclusively positive reviews are a signal about the quality of the manager more than the quality of the team.

Yes, you can have a great team where everyone is contributing well. However, each person still has strengths and weaknesses compared to the role/level rubric. You need to understand that you aren't doing your duty to your team or the company if you don't evaluate people objectively.

Suppose you want to emphasize that the individuals on your team are outperforming individuals on other teams (often crucial if your organization "stack ranks" – creating a forced distribution of employee ratings). Make that point in the accomplishments noted from each team member. Rating your team universally high just looks like you are trying to game the system.

They don't all suck.

Something I see less often is a manager rating their team uniformly poorly, usually when a new manager joins an existing group. When I see this, I wonder if the manager is trying to make a statement about the team they inherited, if they are setting the initial base level low so they can show improvement, or if they are setting their bar way too high. As with overly positive reviews, this behavior is often more indicative of issues with the manager than the team.

If you find yourself compelled to give poor ratings to the entire team, challenge yourself to defend your ratings by comparing each person's accomplishments against the rubric. Are you being to harsh in your judgement or can you justify each of the ratings? Use a "five whys"[42] exercise for each person's rating. Do find unique causes for each person's poor performance, or does it all come back to you?

Use the data you collected and analyzed in your review.

As you fill out the form, answer each question to support your message for the recipient. Answer each question with a statement, then provide data that supports your answer.

Avoid phrases that ascribe intent to the person's actions. Instead, speak to what they did and the measurable effect it had. Do not use expressions like "I think" or "it seems." These phrases show a subjective interpretation. You want to ground your assessment in facts. Being fact-based avoids any disputes about the review if the person does not like the result.

Provide a plan to help underperformers.

Identifying areas of growth for someone is helpful for them. However, if you are being straightforward, a review for someone underperforming can be demotivating. Rather than finding positive things to balance the assessment at the risk of making it less forthright, you should focus on how you will help the person address their performance issues. If the performance is so poor that the person will put on a performance improvement plan, be specific on what they need to change to move off of the PIP.

Provide next steps for growth for the people performing well.

What are the next steps for those on your team who are overperforming against their role/level? What opportunities can you identify for them? What new responsibilities? Are they on a path for promotion? Where should they focus on continuing their growth?

People who are doing well aren't usually satisfied with being recognized for their work (although it is imperative to acknowledge their work). They want to know what is next for them. They want more responsibility, more challenge. They want to expand their skills. How will you help them do that in the next review period? They will want to know.

There is nothing wrong with just doing the job.

Most of your team will not be underperforming or overperforming. They will be doing their jobs well. The work that these folks do is essential. They are how the team's work gets done. Recognize their strengths and weaknesses and tell them how you will support both.

Some are happy to continue to deliver solid performance, and unless your company has an up-or-out culture[43], this is fine. People will have natural ebbs and flows in their careers.

If the person is ambitious, focus on opportunities for their growth and be clear on what overperforming requires. The company's career pathing rubric is a reference to show them what is needed.

When you have written all the performance reviews, reread them.

Once you have completed all the performance appraisals, go back and review them. Look for patterns in your assessments.

Look for potential unconscious bias[44]. Try to read them as your manager or some future manager of the person would. Are you providing enough information to justify your statements? As this process can take a long time, does it seem that you put less effort into later reviews when you got tired?

Before submitting them to your review system, make sure that you are happy with them individually and as a group. If you have time, you may want to wait a few days after writing the last review before you reread them to give yourself some space.

If your review process includes a grade, ranking, or nine-box[45] classification, ensure that your performance reviews support where you put each person. Also, see if the rankings or grades distribution makes sense. For example, are your recommendations so clustered that it doesn't seem that you are using good judgment? Does your review justify your choices?

NOW THAT YOU HAVE WRITTEN YOUR REVIEWS, BE READY WITH YOUR RAISE RECOMMENDATIONS.

In some companies, salary change recommendations are part of the performance review writing process. It runs as a separate process in other companies (usually near the performance review process on the calendar). Line managers do not have direct input into compensation changes at some companies.

However compensation changes work in your company, it is good to understand how to make compensation decisions/recommendations for your team. That is the subject of the next chapter.

CHAPTER 21

Writing Useful Performance Reviews: Making a raise recommendation

Originally published on December 18, 2021

Determining compensation is a crucial part of performance management. I fully believe in the Autonomy, Mastery, and Purpose[46] trio for motivation outlined in Daniel Pink's book **Drive**. However, experience has shown me that even people who have all three of the trio still expect performance in their role to result in more significant compensation.

Aside from hiring or firing an employee, compensation decisions are the most important decisions a manager can make. The decision is significant because the basis for next year's compensation is this year's, especially if you stay at the same company. A manager's mistake in remuneration can result in a significant difference in lifetime salary for someone. Therefore, the compensation change recommendation must be highly considered and fair.

In some companies, the manager creating and delivering the performance review has little input in the compensation decision. If this is your situation, it is still helpful to understand how salary works at other companies, since you may hire people from those places. It is also beneficial when you are responsible for that decision after a promotion.

How does the compensation process work?

Many junior managers have unrealistic expectations around what can be done with compensation because they don't understand that it is part of the greater corporate budgeting processes. As a result, they imagine an infinite pool of money to draw from for raises.

Every company does its budget and compensation processes differently, but there are common aspects across all the companies I have worked at. One generally true statement is that larger companies will typically be more fixed in their processes and make exceptions infrequently.

The compensation budget is part of the larger company budget, which is agreed upon with the board of directors before the start of the year. An essential measure of the ability of the senior leadership team is their capability of working within the constraints of this agreed-upon budget. This budget objective means that at the most senior levels of the company, someone is keeping an eye on the total salary budget for your organization and will work very hard to make sure that it is not over budget. There is a target salary budget for your team based on the team's current salaries and the board's agreed-upon raise budget as a delta.

Your manager will recoup the difference from another team if they allow you to go beyond that budget. Does this mean you shouldn't go over budget if it is warranted? No, but it means you need to have realistic expectations about what is possible.

To avoid budget constraint challenges, line managers in some organizations do not have salary recommendation responsibility.

If you can make salary recommendations for your team, how does the procedure generally work?

You receive:

- your teams' current salaries and some indication of what their most recent raises were,
- an idea of the overall budget target for the organization (usually presented as a percentage delta on existing salaries),
- the salary bands that individuals are currently in, and
- some guidance around the process (possibly including some default raise percentage for different levels of performance).

If you don't receive all this information, you should request it. It is vital for the decision-making process.

You make an initial recommendation for each team member, which you send to your boss. Your manager combines your proposals with those of your peers, adds in their own direct reports (including you), massages the numbers somewhat, and passes it to their boss, who does the same. This process continues to the CEO.

A few weeks (or months) later, you receive the final salary numbers for all your reports to communicate to them, either as part of the performance review or separately. Sometimes the numbers are identical to those you recommended; sometimes they are different. Sometimes your boss knows why the numbers are different, and sometimes they do not.

Equity (stock), bonuses, and salary serve different purposes as part of a compensation plan.

Salary is just one part of a compensation scheme; stock, bonuses (if your company has them), commissions (usually only for the sales team), and benefits are all part of how a company attracts and retains its employees. Each of these elements has a different purpose.

Salary is a direct measure of employee performance. It is to reward someone for doing a good job. Employees who are "high performers" are paid more than others in the role whose work isn't as valuable.

Equity, in the form of stock grants or options, is usually seen as a measure of employee potential. Since these vest over time, they are an incentive for an employee to stay longer. Therefore, you want employees who have a high potential to stay and grow at the company. Some companies also use equity to offset salaries, since the immediate cost to the company is less.

Benefits are often overlooked because they are given equally to all employees, but they can be vital to employee retention. For example, if an employee is interested in developing their skills, letting them know that the company can pay for additional training is a significant statement and may counterbalance a raise that they are not happy with.

When making recommendations around employee compensation, take all the aspects of your company's compensation plan into account. Different elements will be more important at various times to your employees.

What about fixed compensation systems?

Some companies, notably Buffer[47] and Gitlab[48], have adopted fixed formula models for employee compensation and transparency about those models. Company founders designed these models to be fair and reduce bias. I think there is a lot of potential in these models, and the people I know at companies that have them are fans.

Typically, the companies that do fixed compensation systems adopt them very early (instead of switching to them later). The companies are transparent about their compensation, which is critical with a nonstandard model. As such, people generally self-select into those companies. The mechanics of switching to that model seem very difficult to me.

It is worth paying attention to companies using these systems to see how they scale and grow and see if they become the norm.

WHAT IS THE RIGHT RAISE FOR SOMEONE?

The significant part of the fixed compensation systems is that they take the bias and subjectivity out of the raise decision. The bias is all built into the decisions that created the original model. You should strive to be objective and fair for the more standard processes. You should validate the reasoning you use with your manager and peers to ensure that the organization uses a consistent rationale.

Start with their current salary.

Where is the person's current salary within the salary band? Does that current salary make sense, given their past performance? Has the band gone up significantly since the last salary review period? Where do they sit relative to their peers in the same role/level doing similar quality work?

Now think about their performance since the last salary review.

Are they meeting your expectations or exceeding them? Not achieving them? What has been their trajectory over the last few periods? Are they gaining momentum? Losing it?

Is the person being promoted?

If you are promoting the person, you should be gauging them against the bands for their new level. Unless the promotion is long overdue, or the person was very highly paid relative to their peers in their previous level, they should be coming into the lower part of their new salary bands. Placing them in the appropriate spot in the salary band gives them ample room for raises as they grow into their new responsibilities.

Now, look at the target percentage for the organization.

Some of your team should be over that, and some should be under. Your boss will tell you if they expect you to achieve a budget target or not. Even if you anticipate not to come in exactly on budget, you shouldn't be wildly off it. Now, based on the target budget, the person's current salary, and their performance, put in your initial number for them.

If you aren't given a spreadsheet with your team's numbers, you should create one.

I generally have something like this (and create it if I don't get one from the HR team).

	Name	Level	Salary Range Low	Salary Range Mid	Salary Range High	Last Raise	Current Salary	Proposed increase	New Salary
1									
2	Sandy	Senior Eng	50000	67000	80000	5%	65000	0%	65000
3	Morgan	Eng II	20000	28000	35000	4%	29000	0%	29000
4	Skyler	Eng III	30000	45000	55000	3%	47000	0%	47000
5	Jaime	Senior Eng	50000	67000	80000	7%	79000	0%	79000
6	Pat	Eng II	20000	25000	28000	6%	24500	0%	24500
7	Jody	Test Eng I	10000	15000	18000	4%	16000	0%	16000
8									
9									
10					current salary budget		260500		
11					target raise %		5%		
12					new salary budget		260500		
13					proposed raise %		0%		
14									

no, those aren't real people or salaries

A spreadsheet helps you look at your recommendations for people relative to one another, and it enables you to understand what you regard as the target for your team.

As you figure out your initial recommendation for each person, enter it into the spreadsheet.

Don't pay attention to any of the other data while you do this. If it helps, you can hide any rows or columns that you are concerned may throw off your judgment. You can also enter it into another tab if you prefer.

After you have done your first-pass numbers for everyone on your team, you can see where you are relative to your budget. You should also look across the team to ensure you are using consistent logic. It is better to look at percentages rather than salary amounts at this stage. Are the overperforming people relative to your career rubric getting more significant raises than those underperforming or merely meeting expectations? Are the raises going to underperformers in alignment with their performance?

One way to approach this is to think about the raise conversation relative to the performance conversation. Are you saying the same thing with both?

For example, a sizeable raise completely blunts a stern message to someone underperforming. Similarly, a slight raise blunts any positive message in the performance review for an overperformer.

If the raise percentages seem fair, look at the budget total.

Are you over budget? If you are over by a relatively small amount, and your manager has not asked you to be right on target, you may be ready to show them the numbers for their input. On the other hand, if your manager has asked you to be right on budget, then you will need to make some adjustments.

THERE ARE SEVERAL THINGS YOU CAN TRY TO REDUCE THE OVERALL AMOUNT.

If you are significantly over budget, you can use one or more of several techniques for bringing your numbers down.

You may reduce all the raise recommendations by a fixed percentage amount.

Applying the same amount of reduction to all your recommendations keeps them the same relative to one another.

Instead of giving small percentage raises to underperformers, consider reducing them to zero.

If someone is significantly underperforming, recommend no raise rather than giving them an insubstantial raise. Receiving no raise will ensure a difficult review conversation, but it will reinforce the underperformance message.

Decrease individuals' percentages to achieve a rounded salary number.

When given their new salary information, people will look at the percentage and the new salary number and remember one of them, the salary. They won't recollect the exact wage; they will round the number in their heads. Take advantage of that to get some extra headroom.

Let's look at one of our fictional employees, Sandy. Sandy has done very well this year, and you want to reward them with a big raise. Your first idea is a 9% raise, which will give them a new salary of 70,850. After doing the rest of the raises, you are more over budget than your manager is OK with. Since Sandy is your second-highest paid employee and is getting a big raise, you can give them a slightly smaller amount, and they will likely not miss it. Instead, if you gave them an 8.46% raise, that would give them a new salary of 70,500 (a nice round number), and it would save you 350. If you needed more room, 70,250 or even 70,000 are still big raises from their initial 65,000, but are only minor percentage differences from your initial idea.

Robinhooding helps you give more significant raises to lower-paid employees.

The rounding trick I mentioned above is also helpful if you work against budget constraints, but you want to give more significant raises to those on the lower end of the salary spectrum. A small percentage change for a well-paid person can be a very substantial percentage change for someone who is less well-paid. I call shifting small percentages from higher-paid to lower-paid employees Robinhooding.

If you are under budget, should you increase your raises?

The answer to this question will depend on your organizational culture and norms. If this is your first time making salary recommendations, you might ask your manager for guidance. If all your peers come in over budget, and you are under, you may either look fiscally responsible, overly critical, or like an obvious place to find more funding for your peers' excesses. You don't want your team to suffer for other managers inability to meet a budget.

If you are significantly under budget, you may want to reexamine your recommendations, as this would indicate a seriously underperforming team.

Once you are happy with your overall recommendations from an individual and budget perspective, take one last look at them before submitting them to your manager.

Are your recommendations saying something you do not intend? For example, is there one group getting the majority of the large or small raises? Look for your own unconscious biases appearing in the numbers. Once you are fully satisfied that your recommendations indicate the performance of the individuals on your team, submit them to your HR representative or manager for the next phase of the process.

WHAT HAPPENS NEXT?

Your manager may want to review your recommendations with you, or with you and your peers together. Your manager must ensure that each report uses consistent guidelines for their recommendations. They may do this independently or may pull all their manager reports together for a more extensive session (at a previous company, we called this the "Battle Royale").

Come prepared when it is time to review your recommendations with your manager or peers. Preparation should not be problematic if you have followed the recommendations from the previous chapters. The more concrete examples you can provide to justify your proposals, the better.

Your manager will incorporate the input from you and your peers into a larger version of your spreadsheet. They may need to modify some of your numbers to make their numbers work. Your manager will then do a similar review with their peers, and it will go up the levels of the organization, potentially to the senior leadership team. The more information you give your manager, the easier it will be for them to preserve and defend your recommendations. The information you provide them will also give their manager more information.

Once there is agreement on the salary changes for the organization, the finance team updates the numbers in the payroll system. You then receive the final numbers to pass on to your employees.

I discuss the salary and performance review conversations in the next chapter.

CHAPTER 22

Writing Useful Performance Reviews: Delivering the review

Originally published on January 20, 2022

Each review discussion is one of the most important meetings in a person's professional life. The primary goal of the meeting is as a milestone in a career journey. You will give the person an understanding of the progress they have made and insight into how they can get to the next stage of their career.

All the work preparing and writing the performance appraisal can go to waste by delivering the review poorly. I have always found the review conversation the most nerve-racking for me as a manager because that is where you see the effect of your (hopefully) well-considered analysis on the person. And people are... people. The conversation is always a bit awkward, given the stakes for the person receiving the review—but from there, it can go in many unexpected directions. I've had tense, combative conversations with people receiving a very positive review. Conversely, I've had a very unexpectedly genial and optimistic conversation with someone accepting a poor review. Even if you know the person well, the review conversation can be challenging.

Common advice is to give precise feedback to the people who report to you frequently during the year. If you do this, the review itself should not surprise them, as it would be consistent with what you have already said. However, while someone may have heard the feedback, it is another thing to see it written on a piece of paper with a review "score" (if your organization does that) and a salary adjustment connected to that feedback. Even if you are confident that nothing written in the review is new information, the person receiving it may not feel that way.

The best method I've found for having these discussions go smoothly is to come to the meeting prepared, give the person time to digest their review before the dialogue, and structure the conversation itself.

PREPARING FOR THE DISCUSSION

If you have followed the spirit of the process in the previous chapters, you have assembled, organized, and interpreted a lot of data to write the review. This data is also helpful for your preparation and during the conversation itself. Having the information to explain things further if there are questions or disagreements is valuable. Their memory or interpretation of events is sometimes very different than yours or that of their peers.

Read over their review again. Make sure you have the data at hand to support the evaluation you wrote in case there are questions.

If you think the discussion might be tense, you may even want to rehearse the conversation in advance with another dev manager or someone from your company's HR team. I sometimes rehearse challenging messages in the shower, looking for the right way to say something. You may also prepare positive messages to find the best way to say something without ambiguity.

HAVE EMPATHY FOR THE PERSON RECEIVING THE REVIEW.

Think of the performance reviews you have received during your career. Both the good and bad. What made them stand out to you? Was it the review itself or the discussion (or lack thereof)? While the anticipation and the initial excitement of the evaluation are finding out about a promotion, raise, or bonus, and knowing that your hard work was recognized, the thing you will remember long after was the delivery of the information and the discussion that followed.

I've received at least fifty reviews since I started working. I don't remember the numbers or most of the review scores. Still, I remember the manager who hadn't put any thought into the process, the one who made promises review after review that they never kept, and the assessment where a manager made statements that were demonstrably false and, when shown evidence to the contrary, threw up their hands. I also remember the great conversations I had with the best managers I worked for that made me proud of what I had accomplished and excited about what more I could do (and how they would help me).

While you may be nervous about the conversation, the person you speak to is even more so. For you, it is the conversation that is scary. For them, it is the implications of the discussion on their livelihood. So come to the dialogue with that understanding and empathy for their position.

GIVE THE PERSON THEIR REVIEW TO READ BEFOREHAND.

There is always the question of when to let the person read the actual document. Over the years, I have tried it three different ways:

- Handing the person the review after sitting down to the discussion and letting them read it before speaking
- At the end of the review conversation, to read afterward
- Giving the assessment to them the day before or the morning of the conversation

The method that seems to work best is to give the person the assessment to review several hours before the review discussion, saving the actual numbers for the conversation.

When you give the person time to read and process the review document before the meeting, it allows them to prepare for the meeting. It takes some of the person's concerns away because they know what to expect in the conversation itself, which makes the conversation less stressful for them. If they disagree with the assessment, it gives them time to prepare any argument/evidence they wish to present, making it feel less like an ambush. By sharing the review in advance, I have found that the conversation itself is often more substantive and valuable.

THE REVIEW DISCUSSION

Start with a brief introduction.

While you both know why you are there, it is good to start the discussion with some of the broader contexts around the review process and anything around the company's performance that will be relevant to the meeting (like a limited raise budget in a tough economic year). But, unfortunately, that broader context often gets lost in the review conversation itself, which can lead to confusion or misunderstandings.

Don't bury the lede.

If you've given the document to the person in advance, they will join the meeting with an idea of what to expect in the conversation. However, they will still be wondering about the salary numbers. While you may be talking about other things, until the person knows what their salary change is, they will wonder about it. To make the conversation more valuable, I like to share the salary change information or promotion early in the conversation. Once the person knows the most critical information they will receive, they can focus on the more extensive discussion about career development.

Discuss the document.

Discuss each section in the assessment together to make sure that there is a common understanding and agreement. Now is when you might share more details or data around your statements if needed. Do not just ask, "Do you agree with this section?" Instead, make sure they understand your comments, that you have answered any questions they have, and that they either concur with your assessment or at least appreciate your perspective and the data behind your conclusions.

Where to go from here?

If the review conversation is a checkpoint along a career, it is essential to help the person understand where the next checkpoint could be. It is vital in the review conversation to talk to the future and reflect on the past. Now is an excellent opportunity to give hope and support to someone who had a problematic review cycle or inspire someone who has been doing well to achieve even bigger goals.

Hopefully, you have been having regular discussions about the person's career aspirations. The review discussion is the right time to confirm their goals and discuss how you can help them achieve them. What opportunities can you present to them that will help them grow professionally between this discussion and the next review discussion?

Be very careful about making promises that you can't keep. There are many things beyond your control in the review process, like the raise budget, the stock pool, company performance, global economic situations, or a final promotions approval. Even if you had all those things within your control now, you might move on to a new role or new company by the time of the following review. If you make a promise and cannot keep it, you will demoralize the person and lose their trust. So choose your words carefully when talking about the future.

AFTER THE DISCUSSION

Within a few days of the discussion, write the person a note confirming any statements from the conversation, the answers to any questions you didn't have during the dialogue, and the agreed-upon growth plan. If you have a shared agenda for your 1:1s or a list of topics to discuss, make sure that you regularly review any growth plans by adding them as a discussion topic.

PROBLEM SCENARIOS

What if the person disagrees with my assessment?

From time to time, someone will decide that your interpretation of the data is incorrect and, therefore, your review is wrong. When this happens, go over the person's data you collected for the appraisal. If they have some information you didn't receive in the process that causes you to reconsider, don't promise them that you will change the review. Investigate the new information and if you want to change things, discuss it with your manager. This kind of late change rarely happens, however.

If they continue to refuse to accept your assessment, invite them to sit down with you, your manager, and a person from the people team to discuss it. You want the person's concerns heard, but if they don't have any new data, you also want someone in the conversation who will support you.

What if they want to negotiate a different raise?

People will occasionally believe that the salary discussion is a negotiation. I have heard that this is common in a few cultures, but it is not generally done that way. As I discussed in the previous article, the person's new salary is arrived at as part of a long process, and there isn't much—if any—flexibility by the time you deliver the review to the person.

You generally can't change their salary autonomously, so if you agree to reconsider and then you can't change the number, you look ineffectual as their manager. Also, changing their salary will encourage others to try to negotiate in the salary review discussion (the word always gets around when something like this happens).

If someone is unhappy with their raise, discuss what they could do during the next review period to justify making a more significant raise recommendation. But, once again, don't promise anything!

If someone was expecting an entirely unrealistic raise, you might want to share with them a bit about how the salary review process works and help them understand what normal looks like.

What if their friends at other companies got much larger raises?

Occasionally, in the salary review discussion, someone will tell you about their friend who got a 50% raise. They will also tell you about an article they read that says many companies are giving considerable raises to retain employees. Given how charged salaries are as a subject and how competitive the technology industry is for good talent, much disinformation about salaries is constantly circulating.

When faced with these stories, it is worth discussing your company's salary benchmarking process. Help the person understand that there will always be outliers and unusual situations, but express that those are the exceptions and not the norm. It is also worth discussing the non-salary aspects of your company that make it an exciting place to work. Companies often look to salary as their only employee retention tool when it is hard to retain employees because of their culture, lack of growth opportunities, or uninteresting projects.

IF YOU'VE BEEN REGULARLY GIVING FEEDBACK, YOU'VE PREPARED FOR WRITING THE REVIEW, AND YOU'VE PREPARED FOR THE REVIEW CONVERSATION, IT WILL ALMOST ALWAYS GO WELL.

In this chapter, I talk about the many ways the review discussion can go wrong because that can make the whole process scary for many people. It is good to be prepared for the conversation to go in a challenging direction. However, if you have been open with people about their performance and regularly given them feedback, and you talk to them about how you will help them improve their performance, the tough conversations are few and far between.

I usually end the performance review process proud of what each person has achieved and excited about helping them reach their potential. That is my hope for you as well.

CHAPTER 23

Management and Systems Thinking

Originally published on September 17, 2022

"Until managers take into account the systemic nature of their organizations, most of their efforts to improve their performance are doomed to failure."

DR. RUSSELL ACKOFF[49]

I came across a Twitter thread[50] from Rein Henrichs[51] about management, and I thought it also had many good points about systems thinking.

Senior Oops Engineer
@ReinH

A lot of managers, especially those from an engineering background, think that management is about doing stuff: defining rules, policies, and procedures; assigning tasks; creating external incentives; fixing problems.

4:49 PM · Sep 1, 2022

Senior Oops Engineer @ReinH · Sep 1, 2022
But a manager's outcome is the outcomes of the system they manage, and what they do is create and sustain the context in which that system can achieve those outcomes. This is subtle, and doesn't always look like what most people expect managing to look like.

Senior Oops Engineer @ReinH · Sep 1, 2022
The best managers don't look like they're doing much of anything because they've put in motion a system steers itself towards its desired outcomes without requiring their constant intervention. This is difficult to value in a context where individual performance must be measured.

Senior Oops Engineer @ReinH · Sep 1, 2022
So what we get instead, because most of the people evaluating the performance of managers do not know what a good manager looks like and certainly not how to _measure_ it, is a system that values bad managers that flail around a lot but certainly seem to be _doing stuff_.

Senior Oops Engineer @ReinH · Sep 1, 2022
So what we have a system that is incapable of _seeing_ good managers, with exactly the outcomes you might expect.

Senior Oops Engineer @ReinH · Sep 1, 2022
See: Seddon, John. 2019. _Freedom from Command and Control: Rethinking Management for Lean Service_. CRC Press.

> **Senior Oops Engineer** @ReinH · Sep 1, 2022
> But a manager's outcome is the outcomes of the system they manage, and what they do is create and sustain the context in which that system can achieve those outcomes. This is subtle, and doesn't always look like what most people expect managing to look like.
> Show this thread

It caused me to reflect on my approach to systems thinking in the context of technical leadership.

One of the things that helped me the most as an engineering leader was developing a better understanding of systems thinking. When I (or others) use the analogy of "planting a garden" when setting up teams for success, this is what we mean. We are creating the system to enable groups and individuals to do their best work and then allow good behaviors (and results) to emerge. Of course, creating a system takes longer than pushing things down into the organization. Still, it produces more creativity and autonomy in the organization, making it more resilient to change or challenges.

Managers who do not work with this understanding of systems think that management is purely about doing stuff: defining rules, policies, and procedures, assigning tasks, creating external incentives, and fixing problems. This "doing stuff" approach can produce good results in small teams or for a constrained amount of time.

As Rein Henrichs also correctly points out, building a system can be incomprehensible for others in the organization who are not directly involved (especially in other more transactional disciplines). This lack of understanding has often been my biggest challenge as a company's senior engineering leader.

Building a system takes time. If you can get things to a good place where the system is starting to be self-perpetuating, the rest of the organization will see the improvements and become supporters.

Suppose the leadership team is impatient and doesn't understand what you are trying to do. In that case, senior leadership will lean into the quick fixes listed above, re-organization or replacing individuals or trying to "drive accountability" through reductive top-down control mechanisms.

If that happens, you are stuck trying to mitigate the damage and build a longer-term plan to return to your original goals, but it is often a losing battle. This is because the primary culture of the organization has re-asserted itself, and your chance to evolve it has mostly gone.

HOW DO YOU AVOID THAT FATE?

Communicate! Make your plans clear in the hiring process, your initial days in the organization, and throughout the process. Set realistic timelines for improvement and celebrate the successes along the way. When your peers are impatient, refocus them on the plan and the long-term gains you are working towards. Point to the achievements thus far and try to keep their "eyes on the prize."

WILL THIS ALWAYS WORK?

No. It depends on the company's situation and how much pressure there is on the leadership team. If the company is stressed, it might be better to refocus on shorter-term solutions that don't actively detract from what you are trying to build.

My biggest successes in companies were getting the entire organization on board with the system I was working to build. Gaining support for a new system of working is a culture change, and getting backing is contingent on the company wanting to change. If the company is on a "burning platform," a situation where change is required for the company to grow or survive, you will find less resistance. A burning platform also provides the inspiration to persevere if the change is difficult.

My biggest failures trying to build systems were when I did not communicate my intentions clearly or did not get buy-in from the rest of the leadership team, or when I was not effective at communicating the improvements along the way.

Another challenge can be a change (losing a customer or a tough quarter) that puts pressure on the leadership team. In this case, you need to adapt quickly. Hopefully, the system you are putting in place encourages being nimble. You may need to pause the change to the system to focus on shorter-term tactical solutions. To minimize the disruption in the organization, be transparent about the need for the change, and set an expectation on how you will get reoriented towards your original vision afterward.

While there are many good books on systems thinking, the one I consistently recommend for engineering leaders is ***Management 3.0*** by Jurgen Appelo. It isn't just about systems thinking but weaves it into a broader book about management.

Agile

I was exposed to Agile early. In 2000, I was working as a Development Lead at an early-stage startup, Bootleg Networks. The architect, Carmine Mangione, suggested that we try a new development process, eXtreme Programming (XP). I had just left the Windows Media team at Microsoft and was ready to try anything new after six years of Waterfall Development.

The small team at Bootleg produced more useful, working, code in six months than many much larger teams I had been on had produced in multiple years.

I have been a devotee of Agile ever since.

CHAPTER 24

Hiring Agile Coaches

Originally published on June 22, 2020

This tweet from Dave Nicolette inspired me to discuss what I look for when hiring Agile professionals.

Figure 22 - Dave Nicolette Tweet

UNDERSTANDING THE VALUE OF AGILE COACHES

While I have been working exclusively with Agile techniques since we adopted Extreme Programming at a start-up where I was the development lead in 2000, I had never encountered a team-aligned full-time Agile professional before I joined Spotify in 2013. My prior experience with Agile was always that the team was responsible for it.

As a development lead, I was the XP coach when we adopted Extreme Programming. When my teams chose Scrum, I might take the role of Scrum Master, or it was the Program Manager, someone else on the team, or float between multiple people.

When I came to Spotify and found that I had three Agile coaches in my tribe, I was first a bit skeptical about the role. The coaches I worked with were not program managers, not scrum masters. They didn't "lead" Agile in the teams with whom they worked. I wasn't sure what their purpose was.

I first understood their value when one of them went on an extended vacation a few months after I started. At Spotify, I found the most advanced and mature implementation of Agile/Lean product development at a scale I had ever seen. I knew the coaches helped with this, but I wasn't sure how.

The coach went on their vacation, and everything kept going on as usual for a while. I would visit the standups, and teams added stories and tracked them across the boards. One day I sat in on a squad's standup and noticed they had added a couple of swim lanes to their Kanban board. They now had more swim lanes than developers—a big red flag.

Over the weeks the coach was gone, the teams slowly slid into bad habits. Velocity started to slip. I did my best to make them aware of this and get them back onto better paths, but I couldn't be with each team enough.

The coach returned from vacation, and within a week or so, things were back to their high levels of performance. I wanted to see how he did it, so I watched the ceremonies when I could. He didn't cajole or quote Agile texts at them. He gently reminded them what good looked like, lessons they had learned in the past. He asked them questions about their approach. He didn't "fix" them. He got them to fix themselves—a true coach.

Now I understood the value of the Agile coach role.

GOOD COACH, BAD COACH

As Spotify grew and the number of Agile coaches in the company swelled, I also saw some challenges with the role. Some coaches were highly effective, and some less so. I was lucky to start with three excellent coaches on my team. Some of my peers struggled with the coaches in their organizations.

As I came to understand the characteristics of the coaches that I found successful, I started to look for those qualities as we hired into our team. I have continued to look for those qualities as I have created those roles at companies in the US and UK where the role of Agile Coach (versus Scrum Master, Delivery Manager, or Agile Project Manager) is still novel.

Before I enumerate those characteristics, I want to make one point about careers as an Agile professional.

It is a tough job.

In many parts of the world, full-time Agile roles are very hard to come by. Mostly, companies hire Agile folks on a contractual basis. So, most Agile people must string together six- or twelve-month stints at various companies to earn a living.

After reviewing hundreds of US and European resumes, the same companies show up often. These companies are always the ones who are in year X of a one-year Agile transformation program. Those are soul-crushing gigs.

The stringing together of short-term jobs can lead to a consultant mindset. These folks have the wisdom from jumping into hostile environments, trying to survive. They have seen many mistakes that companies have made. Few have held the more extended roles where they have not only got teams functioning in an Agile way but also helped them evolve to a much better level. Their experience is broad but not deep.

It is vital to keep that in mind as you review applicants. You must understand their world and watch out for folks stuck in that short-term mindset.

WHAT I LOOK FOR WHEN I HIRE AGILE COACHES

- **A product development background.** It isn't critical which specific history the person has as a developer, tester, product manager, UX designer, engineering manager... I want to see that they had direct experience shipping a product. Agile roles have been around long enough that there are now schools that train them, and then they go right into the profession. From my experience, Agile people without experience building products can have difficulty making the sometimes necessary trade-offs. They may focus too much on the "how" without understanding the "why," "what," or "when."

- **Broad knowledge of Agile frameworks and techniques.** While the core of Agile thinking has existed for many years, new practices and methods continue to evolve. Like any profession, I look for a candidate to demonstrate that they are not only keeping up but are interested in what is happening in their field.

- **Experience growing a team's proficiency over time.** As mentioned above, many Agile professionals get stuck in an endless series of Agile transformations at different companies. While this is a valuable experience for an Agile consultant, it isn't practical for someone in a long-term role.

- **Pragmatic, not pedantic.** Pragmatism is something I look for in everyone I hire. I would not expect this to be an issue for an Agile professional, but I have interviewed people whose definition of what was or was not correct was defined by a single book.

- **Knowing what good looks like.** The characteristics of a high-performing Agile team are incredibly context-dependent. There is no single way to be an effective team. So how do you convince teams to invest in improvement? You need to give them a vision of what they can be, meaning you need to know what "good" looks like.

- **Knowing what bad looks like.** The converse of knowing what good looks like is knowing what bad looks like. I want to hear what the candidate identifies as harmful patterns in a team. The patterns they identify help me understand how they look at teams. I also want to listen to their techniques for breaking teams out of these patterns. I want to hear what has worked and not worked for them.
- **A desire to build something bigger than themselves.** I want to see some ambition in a coach. Not just to get a group working well but to redefine what a group can achieve with the proper support. If a candidate thinks their job is complete when the team has regular ceremonies, a groomed backlog, and a good flow of tickets, they probably aren't what I am looking for.
- **Experience working with cross-functional stakeholders.** Too many people view Agile as a software development thing, with defined boundaries aligned to the engineering team. Successful Agile organizations interface with the whole company, even if those functions do not choose to work in an Agile way.

BUILDING AN AGILE COACHING PRACTICE IN YOUR ORGANIZATION

If you want to develop a new Agile coaching practice within your organization, it is best to start slow. Hire one coach, and work with them to establish what the role means within your company. When the organization demands more time from them than they have to give, it will be time to hire a second coach, and so on.

Each coach should be able to support multiple teams, especially if you want the teams to own their practices instead of the coach (this is one reason why the coach should not be the scrum master for the groups they work with). Working with multiple groups also helps give some visibility across the organization about the quality of Agile practices and is an excellent conduit for best practice sharing.

You may have over-hired coaches when the Agile coaches start to drive their own deliverables and organize their work as a function. That may mean that the coach-to-team ratio is off.

If you are serious about evolving your Agile practice as an organization and improving your teams' quality, efficiency, and happiness, hire an Agile coach.

But make sure you hire the right one.

CHAPTER 25

Transcript of my speech from OPEX Week Summer 2018

Originally published on August 28, 2018

Author's note 2023: *For a brief period, I found myself welcomed into the operational excellence community. It was a fascinating insight into a world related to my work, but one where efficiency and failure avoidance were the overriding goals instead of speed and innovation. We agilists sometimes like to deride the Six-Sigma crowd, but we owe them a debt, and I appreciated learning more about their work.*

In the software industry today, we can change our product daily in response to direct, instantly measured customer feedback. We can trivially give different versions of our products to different customers to see which they like more. We have figured out how to reduce the time from idea to customer value to revenue from years to days or even hours.

Some of you are thinking, "That would be great to be able to do that in my industry." Some of you are thinking: "What a nightmare, how do you plan, track and manage in that environment?"

The thing is that when I started in the software industry, it didn't work this way. We would spend months designing and planning, then we would build the new product, then we would ship it to customers, and then we would start on the next product. It would take years. If we misjudged our customers' needs, it would take us years to find out and correct the issue.

For software, the revolution of the internet allowed us to break free of our old industrial manufacturing paradigms. It was a two-edged sword because the platform that enabled us to become leaner and more efficient also lowered the bar to competition. The speed of innovation is now a critical aspect of success and survival. Easy access to investment has reduced the value of efficiency to less than zero. Companies can lose money indefinitely if they can show continued growth. If we, the market leaders, become complacent, a much smaller competitor can come from nowhere and take our market away instantly. The barriers to entry are now lowered significantly.

What I am describing may seem interesting, academic, or even obvious to some of you. "That's nice for you" or "Too bad for you over in software," you might be thinking, "but my industry is different." Tell that to the taxis, the automotive manufacturers, or retail.

Just as we in software improved our agile and lean software development processes by learning from TPS[52], Deming, and the established OPEX practices and literature, we can share what we have learned back with the larger OPEX community today.

This talk is short, so I will focus on one way we've found to improve innovation velocity: an authentic autonomy culture.

For me, an autonomy culture starts with Toyota and its' Kaizen.

Kaizen pushes responsibility for improvement through the whole organization and puts the decision-making closer to where the knowledge is. However, the companies I know and have spoken to usually use kaizen to make efficiency improvements to the process, not the product itself.

If you want to bring more innovation into the product, you must find how to bring autonomy to more levels of the organization

- Empowering teams with access to the customer
- Giving them the ability to perform low-risk experiments to validate their hypotheses
- Using data to inform their decision-making and measure their effectiveness

You are changing the model of the organization from plan/command/control to inform/inspire/measure. It's a fundamental culture shift. Leadership sets the direction and high-level strategy, and each team in the levels below figures out how they should approach their part of achieving that strategy with increasing levels of specificity.

The inform/inspire/measure model was how we worked at Spotify, it was how we evolved to function at Avvo, and this will be how we work at AstrumU as we grow.

If hiring smart people, you should take advantage of their intelligence and creativity. If you are not hiring intelligent people, you must consider why you can't trust the people you hire.

For your teams to be successful, they need access to their customers. They need data. Find ways to instrument your product to give data on real-world use back to your teams. If that isn't possible, share the data from your user research, industry and market trends, user testing, competitive analysis, and product focus groups with your whole organization.

Data can also help establish accountability. Work with your teams to develop objective data-driven business metrics for which they can be uniquely accountable. Avoid vanity metrics or non-objective ones. Every team should be able to tie what they do back to the company's core business, even if what they do is support the other teams. Empowering other groups to be more efficient will help drive your core business outcomes.

If your company isn't data-driven today, you may need to train your teams to understand and utilize data. This training will not be a wasted effort.

At Avvo, we created a data-driven decision framework. We trained everyone in the company in its use. It was our version of a Kaizen card. It required the employee to validate their thinking with data and validate their decision's success or failure with data as well. Data became a central part of our processes and discussions as a deliberate side-effect of this effort.

Teams armed with the context they need to make intelligent decisions and tools they can use to measure outcomes objectively against the broader business goals can be given more autonomy.

One more thing is needed, though, before the organization can truly embrace this model: ways to limit the risk of failure. Innovation requires failure. You can't do something genuinely new without making mistakes along the way. If we want our companies to be more innovative, we must reduce the risk of failure. Data reduces risk, but it alone isn't the answer.

You need to find areas where your teams can experiment in the market in limited ways with actual customers. With rapid prototyping tools and limited run manufacturing capabilities, this has become increasingly easy over the last decade. Giving teams this ability lets them experiment and learn rapidly by giving them the knowledge they need. In turn, they can innovate without putting the whole company at risk.

What of governance, compliance, oversight, quality, and process control? These things are still as vital as ever, but how they function will need to evolve in an autonomous enterprise. They must be integrated and intrinsic, part of the DNA so that teams naturally incorporate them into their experiments. For the areas where this is most critical, the groups may need that expertise integrated into the team structure instead of externally applied.

I discuss this with you as a thought exercise, a different way of approaching innovation in your organization. It is working wonders for us in the software industry. I have spoken with high street banks in the UK, large department stores in the

Netherlands, multi-national financial institutions, heavy equipment manufacturers, personal grooming appliance makers, and others looking into these ideas of autonomous teams to bring more innovation into their practices.

If it is possible for them, then it is entirely possible for you.

Thank you

Leading Organizations

Transitioning from being an individual contributor to a team manager is challenging. Growing from managing a team to a set of teams to an organization is substantially more difficult, especially if the organization is growing quickly.

The lessons I learned that helped me be an effective leader of a forty-person organization held me back as my team grew to seventy-five and then one hundred people. I had to take a completely different approach.

Once I learned to recognize when my existing tools were no longer serving me and how to build new tools when needed, I could be an effective leader for organizations of one hundred and seventy-five or more people.

This section shares some of those lessons and tools.

CHAPTER 26

The Spotify model: how to create, dissolve, and remix teams to be more dynamic and more innovative

Originally published on January 6th, 2015

One of the most challenging parts of managing a traditional, hierarchical, organization is being responsive to new opportunities; especially those that require leveraging skillsets outside your own team. At Spotify, our organizational model allows us to create, dissolve, and remix teams with minimal disruption to individuals or managers. This gives us tremendous abilities to address both temporary and long-term opportunities.

HOW IT USED TO BE

As a manager at Microsoft and Adobe, I was always challenged when there was a problem or opportunity that required repurposing a team or adding on additional scope to an existing team.

This kind of thing comes up all the time: a business development opportunity, or integration with another product. Often, this would require small efforts from multiple specialized teams.

It would cause disruption as those teams had to change their current plans and coordinate around a new challenge while still making progress towards their existing goals. Given that people and resources were managed within the team, and managers were still responsible for delivery of their existing commitments, often it would be hard to motivate them towards supporting this new effort.

Creating a new "tiger" team is often the solution in these situations, but that isn't always an adequate solution for long-term or permanent projects since it essentially punishes the managers of the existing teams and requires finding a new temporary manager for the new team.

Another problem in existing organizations is figuring out what to do with a team whose project has been canceled.

If the team is a high-performing team you may try to turn the team onto a new problem, which may or may not be a good fit for their skills and experience. You may instead dissolve the team, assigning the members to new teams based on the needs of those teams rather than the preferences of the individuals. You may leave it up to the individuals to find new roles in the company or face layoffs if they are unsuccessful.

These solutions end up punishing both the individuals on the teams and their managers, often for reasons beyond their control. In an organization seeking to innovate (which requires some amount of failure), it sends a counter message to one of experimenting and taking chances.

HOW WE REMIX TEAMS AT SPOTIFY

At Spotify, we wanted to create an organization that allowed us to be dynamic around our staffing, and adaptable in our teams.

We embrace failure as being important to learning and innovation, so we didn't want dissolving a team to be a punishment. We put this new organizational model into effect over two years ago and have been working with it since. In that time, the technical organization has grown from 250 to over 600 people. We went from having three engineering offices to five, and from having 30 teams to over 70.

We focused on building full-stack, autonomous teams, built around a single, clear, mission. The expectation is that it will dissolve once the team's mission has been fulfilled.

To this end, new teams are constantly being created and old teams dissolving, with their members building new teams or moving into existing teams if they need additional staffing. Rather than create a formal manager role for these teams, we decided instead to make the teams collectively responsible for fulfilling their mission.

With this model, changing teams does not mean changing your manager, and dissolving a team doesn't leave a manager looking for a new role.

We do have a strong belief in the role of the manager as a mentor to their reports, so we have a strong managerial culture; it is just manifested in a matrix, rather than a hierarchical model.

WHY CHAPTER LEADS WORK BETTER THAN TRADITIONAL MANAGERS

Our technical managers are called Chapter Leads. They are usually responsible for managing a narrow range of developer disciplines within their larger organizations, for example: mobile developers, or backend developers. A Chapter Lead usually has direct reports in multiple teams in the organization.

For an individual, it is common to change teams, but it is less common to change managers. As each team is responsible for their full stack and all platforms, a team may include members from several chapters.

An example is the search team in my organization. Its members come from five different chapters: the backend chapter, the mobile chapter, the keyboard and mouse (desktop and web) chapter, the agile coach chapter, and the test chapter. Additionally, there is a product owner and a UX designer, both of whom are part of the product organization (which is organized more traditionally).

The Chapter Leads are not responsible for deliverables directly. Instead, the Chapter Leads are responsible for staffing the teams appropriately, for working with the individuals in the team to help them grow; and for working with the Product Owner and the Agile Coach to make sure that the team is performing well together.

Since the Chapter Lead has visibility into multiple teams, they can often identify short or long-term skill set needs and are empowered to resolve them.

Sometimes, this means switching two developers in two teams temporarily for a skill set need. Sometimes, this means moving a developer to a different team to address a short-term staffing need. This also means that if there is a new mission to be addressed, the chapter leads can work together to staff a new team to address that mission out of the existing teams in the organization.

A benefit of this model for an individual is that there are many opportunities for them to work on new projects or develop new skillsets since there are new projects spinning up on a regular clip.

WHEN AND HOW WE REMIX AND DISSOLVE TEAMS

This remixing is not constant throughout the technology team. We do have several very long-lived teams that are focused on features in the product, but even those teams will shift people between each other based on short or long-term needs. In some parts of the organization, specifically the infrastructure teams, they tend to be focused on short-term projects and are creating new teams more often. Those teams dissolve when they have completed their project.

We will also dissolve teams if we believe their mission is no longer necessary. Usually, this is the result of the team invalidating their mission themselves. We celebrate these conclusions just as much as the successful completion of the project since we value the lessons from a "failed" project. Celebrating your failures as valuable lessons encourages risk-taking, experimentation, and innovation.

By striving towards a model that gives the individual consistency (their manager, and their Chapter) while still offering the organization fluidity and adaptability, we've found a happy balance that lets us extend our agile-first values beyond the work that a team performs to the organization as a whole. This has allowed us to focus on innovation and leverage opportunities that slower-moving organizations would have difficulty addressing.

Several companies have attempted to adapt our model, but there is something critical to understand. Our organization model is fluid and continues to change and evolve to support its needs. The specifics of our implementation are less important than the underlying values and ideals that created it.

If you want the benefits of a dynamic organization, you will need to build something suited to your organization's values. I would argue that a central requirement is endowing teams with autonomy and decision-making authority. If you cannot support this, then you should look instead to adapt your existing model to remove impediments and bottlenecks instead.

CHAPTER 27

Thoughts on emulating Spotify's matrix organization in other companies

Originally published on March 14, 2014

I was in San Francisco in December (2013) for a conference. While there, I connected with a few companies inspired by Henrik Kniberg and Anders Ivarsson's whitepaper "Scaling Agile at Spotify"[53], who have been trying to implement some of those ideas in their own companies.

I think Henrik's paper does an excellent job of describing the what and how, but it seems that the "why" and some critical ideas can get lost when others read it.

If you haven't read Henrik's white paper, I suggest reading it before reading the rest of the chapter. I will do a quick recap here, in any case.

Spotify's engineering and product organization (now over 600 people) is split into several large groups called Tribes. Each Tribe is responsible for a set of related features or engineering functions. For example, our largest tribe is the Infrastructure and Operations Tribe, whose name is self-explanatory. I am the Tribe Lead of the Music Player Tribe. We handle importing audio from our label and distribution partners, storing and streaming the music, search, collection and playlists, artist pages, music metadata, and the music knowledge graph that supports things like the above, but also ads, discovery, radio, and the like.

While the whole company works on the same product, Spotify, each tribe is set up to work as independently as possible. As you will see below, a critical aspect of our organizational model is to give autonomy at every level. This autonomy helps remove decision-making bottlenecks and unnecessary dependencies, which improves velocity.

Each tribe is composed of squads. A squad is a team responsible for a single feature or component. For instance, among the teams, one is dedicated to handling searches while another manages the AB test infrastructure, among other specialized squads. We set up each tribe and squad to function as autonomously as possible. In the context of a feature development team, each must be full-stack. A full-stack team is responsible for both back-end implementation as well as user interface implementation on all platforms.

A typical feature squad would have web service engineers, iOS, Android, web, and desktop engineers, as well as testers, an agile coach, a product owner, and a UX designer. With this staffing, the squad has everything they need to implement anything related to their feature. They don't have to wait for another team to implement the necessary pieces. They also have autonomy and local decision-making ability, so there are few impediments to their speed of execution.

To this point, with Tribes and Squads described only, Spotify may seem like a traditional, hierarchical engineering organization, but this is where the similarity ends. Unlike a traditional organization, a squad does not have a single engineering leader whom everyone on the team reports to. In fact, there is not a single leader for the squad. The Product Owner and UX Designer collectively work with the engineers and testers to make decisions about their features.

Spotify is not a "no manager" culture, however. We strongly feel that managers have a role in supporting the people who work for them. Managers are essential as technical and career mentors and organizational communication conduits. Rather than have management hierarchies follow organizational ones (creating a de facto command-and-control structure), we instead have first-level managers responsible for technical functional areas across multiple squads.

We call these reporting and functional groupings "chapters." Again, as an example, reporting to me, the tribe lead, are Chapter Leads. In my tribe, there are currently three backend (services) development chapters, two front-end development chapters (including all the UI developers), a core library chapter, and a test chapter. These seven Chapters span eight different squads. Almost every chapter lead has reports in two squads, and a few have direct reports in three. Nearly all chapter leads work within a team in some capacity as well, either as a developer or technical lead, and not necessarily within a squad with members of their chapter.

This chapter/squad matrix organization is critical to our organizational agility. It allows the squads and the tribe to be more fluid. We can spin up a new squad to take advantage of an opportunity or handle an issue without worrying about changing reporting structures. If a squad completes its goals and no longer has a reason to exist, we can dissolve it without punishing a manager. This variance is a significant difference to a traditional hierarchy because it gives us much flexibility and helps us avoid the old political issues around empire-building and resource contention.

In addition to our Tribes, Squads, and Chapters, we also have virtual organizations called Guilds. Guilds are cross-tribe organizations centered on different technical or interest areas, and their membership is voluntary. The guilds serve as ways to promote cross-tribe collaboration and communication, especially around things like best practices. For instance, we have guilds dedicated to a range of areas, including Web Development, Agile Practices, Leadership, and Test Automation, among others. The guilds foster developer-to-developer communication, which is one of the ways that we keep all these autonomous teams from going in entirely different directions.

From Henrik's paper, this diagram illustrates the organizational structure I discuss above:

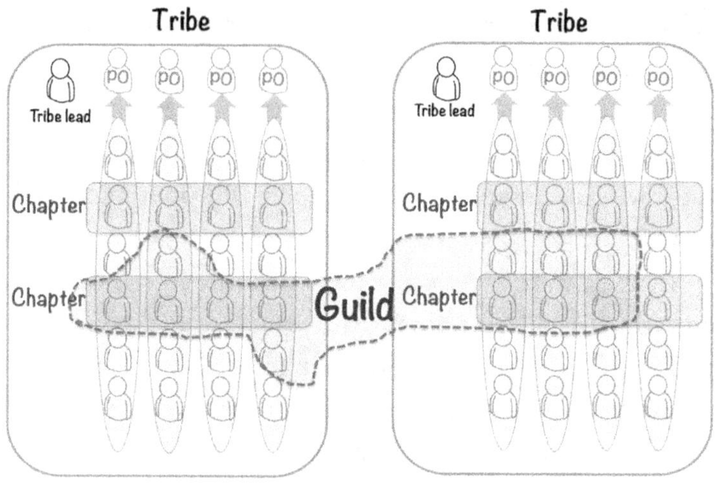

Figure 23 - Spotify Model Matrix Organization
Henrik Kniberg/Anders Ivarsson

I want to give some more background about why we have implemented this organizational model at Spotify, elaborate on our goals for implementing it, and discuss the aspects of our culture that have been critical to its success. It is remarkable that the way we work inspires other companies. Still, if you implement only parts of the model or try to impose it on a very different corporate culture, you will have difficulty achieving the same level of success that we have had.

If you are considering using the Spotify organizational model within your company, there are a few things that will be critical to your success:

Our organizational model assumes that engineering uses agile methodologies. Our goals for autonomy mean that we do not prescribe any particular development framework that our squads must subscribe to. However, all of the teams use agile development methodologies. While we do our best to minimize dependencies between squads and tribes, there will always be some since we are all working on the same product. Any individual squad choosing to build using a traditional waterfall or another non-agile process would be unable to keep up with the rapidly changing teams around them. If they tried to impose some sort of process on other groups so that they could follow a longer-term development plan, they would start slowing down the rest of the organization.

A critical requirement in making our organization model work well is that the entire company works with and understands agile practices and processes. For example, while our legal team isn't doing scrum or kanban, they work with engineering teams that use agile methods. Having the entire corporation understand and agree with Agile means that no line of business area impedes the speed of implementation. Think of this in terms of Amdahl's law[54] applied to a development organization. Suppose your development teams work quickly in parallel, but marketing or legal does not support an agile approach. In that case, they will become a bottleneck that will slow down the overall speed of the company.

Similarly, implementing this with just one team as a test in a larger engineering organization will be prone to issues. Traditional engineering organizations usually don't set themselves up for autonomy. Adding a single autonomous team within that web of dependencies will likely hamper and frustrate that team and skew the experiment's results.

While I've mentioned autonomy in several places, I cannot understate its criticality. We must empower each squad to make their own decisions, encompassing features, the development model, infrastructure, and implementation. Every decision requiring outside approval means a delay that slows development. Each dictated implementation or infrastructure decision means a technology that doesn't fit the way the team works or something new to learn before the team can build. This autonomy is a challenge to coordination, but it isn't as bad as it might seem in practice. Best practices and technologies spread from team to team through avenues like guilds. Teams adopt these practices and technologies on their schedule or pioneer new ways of working if it makes it easier for them to deliver value to our customers and then spread their learnings to the other teams.

Attempting to layer the tribe and squads model over a traditional reporting hierarchy would be very problematic. While we have many long-lived squads at Spotify, we are constantly creating and disbanding squads as new needs arise or the teams fulfill their missions. Squad membership will also ebb and flow as required by the needs of a squad's mission. Traditional hierarchical organizations are self-perpetuating, and restructuring them is very disruptive to the management chains and the individual team members. You would gain some of the benefits of the Spotify model by building full-stack teams in a traditional organizational hierarchy, but you would lose many of the overall speed benefits that we leverage with our matrix organization.

In conclusion, if Spotify's organizational model inspires you and you desire to improve the speed of your product development, there are a few things that you need to understand. Our model works because it is layered on top of our corporate culture. Our culture values autonomy, agile processes, democratic teams, and servant leadership, amongst other things. You can certainly take some of the ideas from how we work and apply them in your organization, but you may not get the same returns without the cultural underpinnings.

CHAPTER 28

Using Self-Selection to Create Journey Teams at Avvo

Originally published on December 9, 2018

Many companies are interested in experimenting with self-selection to organize their teams. I see questions about the process often in online forums. While there are some excellent books and blog posts on the topic, I thought I would share a self-selection exercise we did at my last company, Avvo. It worked well and with relatively little drama. If you are considering a similar exercise, you might consider this approach.

I joined Avvo as its' CTO in the summer of 2016. At the beginning of 2017, we moved to a new team structure. The basis of the new team structure was the customer journeys through our product. The new teams were naturally called "Journey Teams."

I describe Journey Teams briefly in my talk "Building a Culture of Continuous Improvement in Your Company.[55]"

Traditionally, at Avvo, the leadership organized the development teams top-down. I had heard from the individual developers some frustration at how they were placed into teams and moved without consultation. I decided that this re-organization was an excellent way to demonstrate the more inclusive and autonomous culture that I was building. Allowing people to self-select their new team seemed a perfect way to break from the past and set expectations for the future.

PREPARATION

We decided on six Journey Teams. Four were product-focused, supporting customer journeys. The other two were internally focused. One Journey Team supported our developers with tooling to help them manage their services. The other internal journey team focused on supplying business analytics to the marketing, finance, and sales teams.

If someone chooses a team, they need to understand what the team is and why they would want to join it. With our direct reports, the Chief Product Officer and I set the number and charters of the Journey Teams.

Once we set the number and missions of the Journey Teams, we picked an initial leadership group for each team. That leadership group consisted of one senior member of each functional specialty that would be part of the team. The product teams each had a Product Manager, a Development Lead, a Test Lead, a UX Lead, a Data Engineering Lead, and a Data Analytics Lead.

The new Journey Team leadership groups were each responsible for setting up the initial scaffolding of their teams. The scaffolding included: fleshing out their missions, establishing their spheres of responsibilities, putting together some initial strategies they would use, and choosing their core metrics. As they progressed on these, they would review with each other and the senior product and technology leadership. We needed to ensure that every part of the product and platform had an owner and that the plans and metrics made sense.

As the Journey Team leadership groups made progress in building their plans, they put together staffing estimates on what they would need to execute their strategies. The staffing estimates were valuable as they helped me decide what staffing I would need in the next year's budget. The budget process was happening in parallel with this effort.

As we moved into December 2016, the leadership of each of the Journey Teams had made enough progress that I felt comfortable setting the self-section exercise right after the New Year's break in January. At this point, the board had approved the budget. The CPO and I could determine what staffing we would allocate to each team based on their mission and strategy. Each Journey Team then needed to think about how they would structure their efforts based on their assigned staffing.

THE EXERCISE

The self-selection exercise structure was a job fair with a festive atmosphere. The entire product, design, development, test, data engineering, and data analytics teams assembled. We had cupcakes and drinks. One by one, each Journey Team leadership group came up to pitch their team to the rest of the organization. They described their mission, goals, initial plans, and the planned size of the team. Some had already designed logos and slogans. Each team was selling their mission to their peers. Some teams put a lot of effort and salesmanship into their pitches. Other groups had a difficult time articulating why people should join them.

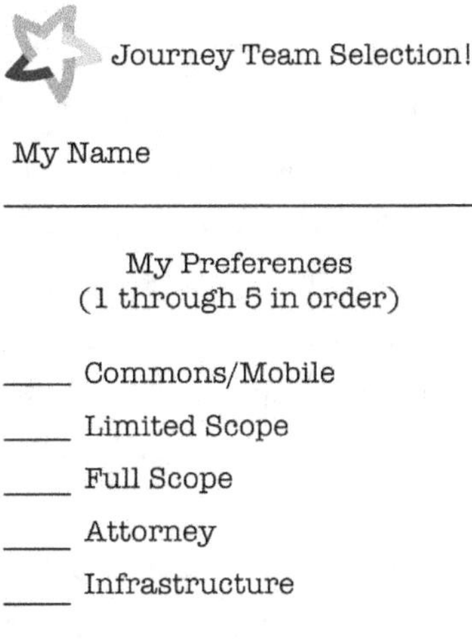

Figure 24 - The Journey Team Selection Card

After the last Journey Team had presented, every person in the room got a card. The card contained a space for their name and a list of the Journey Teams with areas to put their order of preference. We asked everyone to rank their choices entirely, just in case we would need them.

When all the cards were filled out and collected, the meeting adjourned.

FINALIZING THE SELECTION

After the self-selection meeting, the people managers from the organization met. The responses from each card were now in a spreadsheet showing each person's preferences, the number of people currently assigned to each Journey Team, and the number of people budgeted to be on the team.

The people managers were part of the process because they knew their reports' interests, challenges, growth plans, and interpersonal issues. They were there to advocate for their employees' wishes. They were also there to understand the process. With an understanding of the process, they could explain to someone why they didn't get their first choice. The people managers helped to ensure that each team had the best diversity of skills, backgrounds, and experience so that they would have the highest chance of succeeding.

The process of matching people and teams was iterative. As the teams started to fill in, we had to go back and re-adjust a few times. The task of matching people and groups went relatively quickly, only about 90 minutes for a 120-person organization. Along the way, we shifted one headcount between teams to accommodate a developer's professional development interests.

We matched 99% of the people to their first or second choice of Journey Team. In the case where someone got their third choice, we had a reasonable explanation for them about the decision.

Once we set the initial rosters for each Journey Team, the individuals had a chance to review and give feedback. For the cases where people didn't get their first choice, their manager could discuss it with them in their 1:1s.

While we were open to further iteration to accommodate any concerns, it turned out that it wasn't necessary. The Journey Teams and individuals were all content with the matching.

A week after the self-selection exercise, we sent out the official announcement of the new team rosters. The teams started meeting to flesh out the initial plans, and individuals moved to sit with their new teammates. We made it clear to everyone that if they were unhappy with their decision, we would help them switch.

A Retrospective on the exercise a few weeks later found very high satisfaction from the organization with the process and the teams it produced.

THE RESULT

The exercise itself was a success. It had tremendous engagement from the organization. People felt empowered in the activity and committed to their new team because it was their choice. Only one person switched teams in the three months after the exercise and only a handful in the rest of the year.

WHAT I WOULD DO DIFFERENTLY NEXT TIME

The process of preparing for the exercise from each of the Journey Teams created some tension in the organization. The Journey Team leadership groups spent much time meeting together in the weeks before the meeting. The groups weren't transparent enough about what they were doing. We, as leaders, hadn't set reasonable expectations about communication. We started encouraging them to send updates to the organization on their progress, but it came later than it should have. Next time, I would give more guidance to the leadership teams about how they could go about their initial organizing. I would put tighter time expectations on them and ensure they were transparent to the rest of the organization.

The presentations themselves were a bit of a challenge for some teams. We did encourage groups to make their presentations fun and to sell their missions. We didn't help the teams with their presentations, though, and we didn't do a run-through with them. The disparity in presentations did mean that some groups attracted an inordinate amount of interest. Next time, I would have a run-through where each group could see each other's presentations, and we could give some advice to help improve their presentations.

REGULAR SELF-SELECTION EXERCISES

Some in the organization were so happy with the self-selection exercise that they suggested we repeat it every year. I know that there are organizations that do this. From my experience, I can see it working within a small company where almost everyone already has a good connection with each other. Going through the forming, storming, and norming[56] phases in a smaller organization would take much less time. In a larger organization, regular re-organization would mean much wasted time trying to get teams going.

For Avvo, the self-selection made sense at a juncture when we were doing a complete organizational restructuring. The old teams were utterly gone. It took a while for the new teams to get going, but once they established themselves, they worked well, and it made little sense to change them again. Individuals always had the option to move between teams if they felt ready for new challenges. The organization was growing, and so the teams were always hiring. If we had been in a more constrained environment, we would still have done our best to facilitate smooth movement within the organization.

The core thing with an exercise like self-selecting teams or any other activity is to be deliberate in your intent. Why are you doing the exercise? What benefits do you expect? What are the downsides? If it is successful, what will you do next? How will you roll it back if it is unsuccessful, or what will you do instead?

CONCLUSION

Letting the people in your organization self-select into teams can be an active driver of engagement and autonomy. The exercise we did at Avvo was successful for us and is worth looking at as inspiration for your process. If you are considering self-selection, be deliberate about your goals, what aspects of self-selection help you achieve them, and what you might do if the goals are unmet.

CHAPTER 29

Building a Management Training Curriculum at Avvo

Originally published on October 5, 2017

This week, we kicked off manager training for Avvo technology managers. Before building a curriculum, we needed to decide what was essential to learn and where we as a group needed the most development.

If I had done this with my organization at Adobe years ago, I might have made a list of capabilities or requirements for our roles and then assessed each person against those requirements. I've since learned that the top-down approach tends to isolate and alienate people. It is something done TO them. They don't feel investment or ownership of the process. If they disagree with the list or my assessment of them, it is hard to challenge due to the nature of the process.

At Spotify, I worked with Paolo Brolin Echeverria and Mats Oldin to build manager training for my Tribe. They developed an excellent kick-off exercise that I repurposed for my team at Avvo.

The process is straightforward.

We began by individually thinking about the qualities of a good leader in our organization. We each wrote every important quality we could think of onto individual post-its. This effort took about 20 minutes. Then, one by one, we put each of our post-its onto a large board. As we placed each quality, we explained why we believed it was important for a leader at Avvo.

Figure 25 – Kyle Adding Post-Its

When we finished putting all our post-its on the board, we affinity-grouped them. Affinity-grouping resulted in 30 groups of similar qualities and a few individual post-its that did not fit into any group. The grouping process required much more discussion so that we could all agree on the final groupings.

Figure 26 - Nic, Ian, and Jordan working
on cleaning up the affinity groups

At this point, we had collectively described 30 essential qualities of a leader at Avvo, which is far too many to focus on effectively. To narrow things down, we each received six votes to put towards any group of qualities we felt were the most critical. Then, we tallied the votes and took the top eight as our core qualities of a manager at Avvo.

The voting process also led to many valuable discussions as we saw where we had voted as a group. Were these the right eight qualities? Were they the most significant eight?

The eight qualities that we picked were:

- empathy
- develops autonomy
- builds good teams
- is real and trustworthy
- is a big-picture thinker
- supports mastery
- gives feedback
- has a bias for action

Figure 27 - Dot voting in progress

Individually, we then assessed ourselves against the eight core qualities on a three-point scale: "I need training on this," "need training, but it can wait," and "I can train others on this." One by one, we went up to a board with the eight qualities mapped on a spider graph. We put dots on a line for each quality where we rated ourselves. We explained why we chose that assessment. This exercise led to a further discussion about assessing ourselves against these qualities.

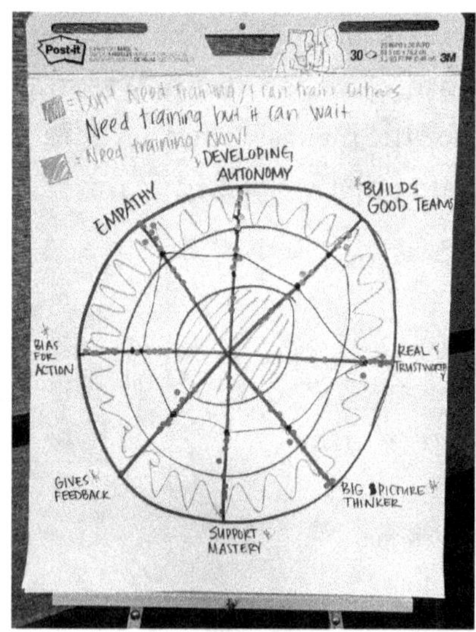

Figure 28 - Our collective spider graph

The group found this exercise to be very valuable. We had excellent discussions on what it means to be a good leader at our company, including the values we agree on and those we don't. We also prioritized the values collectively so that everyone feels ownership and allegiance to them.

And we came to an understanding of where we need to develop the most as a group. This mutual understanding will inform the curriculum for our management training — my original goal.

CHAPTER 30

A diversity challenge: tech start-ups have a great opportunity

Originally published on May 16, 2017

For decades, we've been complaining about the lack of diversity in the technology industry. We've worked on the pipeline problem. We've worked on reducing bias in hiring. We've worked on the sourcing problem. We've worked on the retention problem. The net result thus far is that we've barely moved the needle.

Most of the companies that are investing in diversity programs are large companies. For them, their continuing lack of diversity is a public embarrassment.

At scale, though, it is a far more difficult challenge for a company like Google, Microsoft, or Facebook to reach any percentage of the tech workforce that mirrors their customer base. The numbers are too large to move the needle. It's far easier for startups.

A critical part of building an inclusive culture that supports diversity is reducing "otherness." Inclusiveness is also much harder to do in a large company. If Google hired 1000 developers of color across all their offices, those individuals might never encounter another person like themselves on a daily or weekly basis. They may still be the only person of color their peers see at work. They will be spread too thinly across the population.

Large technology companies should still work consistently to improve their diversity, but startups are much better suited to solve the diversity problem for the industry as a whole.

A startup with a development team of ten, four women, has a ratio of 40% female developers. Any woman who interviews with the company will see that they are welcome. Any man interviewing will understand that they will be joining a company that takes diversity seriously and will be expected to conduct themselves appropriately. This would be the same for any other underrepresented group. If the company is serious about building a diverse workforce, they will find it easier to continue to be diverse as they grow.

Bringing in a diverse workforce at the early stages of a company will also mean leadership opportunities for those employees as the company grows. It will help address the lack of diversity in industry leadership, which further helps build minority representation. It will also eventually mean more startups started by underrepresented industry groups, which will continue to fuel diversity in the industry. Some of these startups may be acquired, putting their leadership into the leadership of other companies, increasing diversity in them.

Most surveys show that startup founders' most significant challenge is hiring development talent. Meanwhile, there are ever-larger numbers of coding schools and boot camps graduating eager junior developers, willing to work hard, and coming from largely underrepresented populations in the industry. Many experienced minority developers at larger companies would be interested in an environment that allows them to be themselves.

Unfortunately, most startups neglect the critical cultural aspects of building their company as they chase product/market fit, funding, or customers. Many haven't considered that building a diverse company will help them find the right product for mainstream audiences, that sources of capital increasingly value diversity in their funding decisions, and that diverse teams build better products that attract more customers.

So, I call on my fellow startup CTOs and CEOs to take on this challenge. If we succeed, we will not only build a better industry but also create better companies for our shareholders, employees, and ourselves.

CHAPTER 31

Changing Hiring Practices to Build a More Diverse Technology Organization

A Case Study from Avvo

Originally published on June 12, 2020

INTRODUCTION

I was the Chief Technology Officer at Avvo from 2016 until 2018 when the company was acquired. Building a more diverse and inclusive technology team was one of the proudest achievements of my tenure there.

Given current events, I hear from friends at tech companies that they are re-evaluating their lack of diversity. They want to improve. While companies have tried different tactics for years, we haven't made much progress as an industry. It is daunting if you are trying to address diversity for the first time. It is easy to try some things, make no progress, and then give up.

This chapter isn't a prescription for improving diversity at any technology company. It is a case study of how we grew diversity at Avvo. The different strategies we employed may be helpful for your efforts. They may inspire you to try new things appropriate for your company and culture.

STARTING POINT

Avvo is an online legal marketplace connecting consumers and attorneys in the US. The company overall was reasonably diverse from both a gender and a race perspective. When I joined in 2016, the technology team was a different story.

The technology organization was not very diverse at the start of my tenure, as displayed in the charts below. Additionally, there was no one from any under-represented groups with management responsibilities in the Technology team.

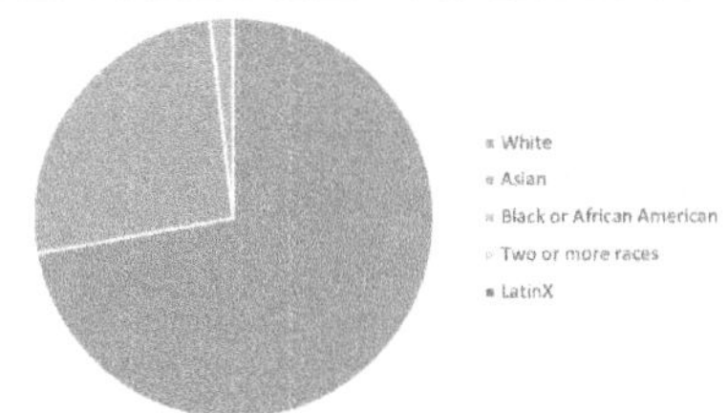

Figure 29 - Avvo Technology Team Racial
Diversity in 2016

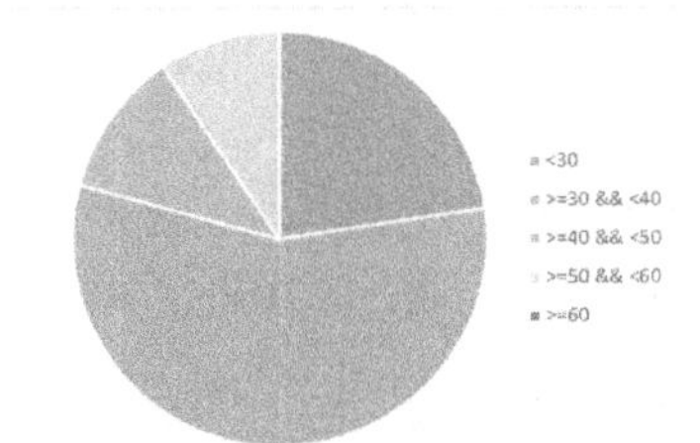

Figure 30 - Avvo Technology Team Age
Diversity in 2016

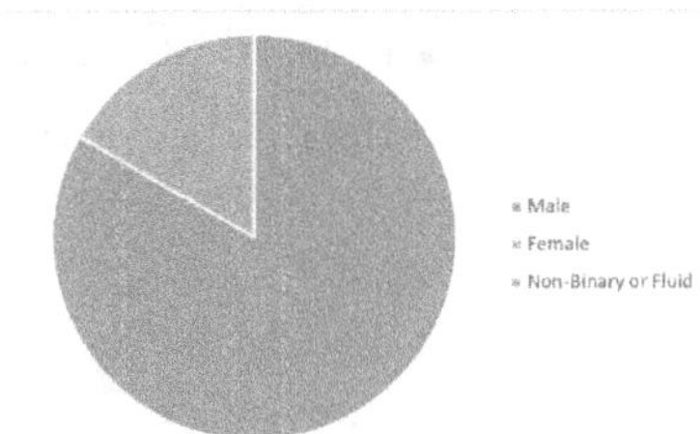

Figure 31 - Avvo Technology Team
Gender Diversity in 2016

The team's status quo was not the result of overt discrimination, but it did demonstrate a lack of prioritization of diversity, inclusion, and reducing unconscious bias.

My vision for the company was to make it an exemplar of diversity and inclusion within the region. I wanted to not only make Avvo's technology team diverse to prove that it was possible, but I also wanted to show that a diverse group is more than capable. I additionally believed that we could use our diversity as part of our employer branding, helping us stand out in a crowded talent market.

MAKING IMPROVING DIVERSITY A PRIORITY FOR TECHNOLOGY

I set the tone I intended to take as part of my interview process for the Chief Technology Officer role. I didn't want any potential for disputes between the rest of the senior leadership and myself.

Once I had accepted the job, I had a multiple-month notice period with my former company. I used the time to talk to the Director of Engineering and head of recruiting to prioritize diversity in hiring, set expectations, and start building a better pipeline.

Building a Coalition and Setting Expectations

If you are working to build a more diverse team, you must get recruiting as your partners in on the effort. While it may seem natural, it is not. Recruiting (especially external recruiters) are incentivized or measured on their ability to close roles as quickly as possible. Most recruiters I have worked with are delighted to help find diverse candidates, but it is critical to let them know you understand that it means it will take the whole process longer. It is also essential that their managers understand this.

If you have hiring managers reporting to you, you need to get them on board and excited about this effort as well. One measure of a manager is their ability to hire well. Being serious about diversity will likely mean they will take longer to fill roles for their team.

You may need to assure them you will consider this if they miss their KPIs (Key Performance Indicators). You cannot set up or hold conflicting goals for your managers. You will likely fail at both if you cannot prioritize building diverse teams over hitting KPIs.

One way to handle the increased hiring time is to start sourcing for a role much earlier than scheduled. Spend the time before the position is scheduled to open only looking at under-represented candidates. Create an agreement with your manager that you can hire ahead of schedule if you find a suitable candidate early. If you reach the planned opening date for the role and haven't located anyone, you can open the pool to your normal channels without losing time.

Your manager will also need to understand the potential impact of a diversity hiring focus on your KPIs.

With your manager's support, create a reasonable KPI or OKR as your goal to track your efforts. The OKR should give you a target and some cover if there are challenges to some of the tradeoffs you may need to make because you are hiring more slowly. Share your goal with your team. Update them on your progress regularly. Transparency is essential but also helps to enlist the rest of your team to do their part to help achieve the goal.

At Avvo, my diversity goals were part of my OKRs. I shared our progress with a monthly update to the organization. This repeated communication demonstrated the level of importance I placed on this goal and showed our improvement in real time.

The good news is that as you progress towards your goal, your time-to-hire will come down while maintaining or increasing your diversity. It does get easier. You will soon stop making tradeoffs as you continue to improve.

FIXING THE INTERVIEW PROCESS

When I joined Avvo, the hiring process involved multiple pre-interviews, a do-at-home coding challenge, a review meeting, an in-person interview loop, and a follow-up meeting. The process may have taken a single candidate over a month to get from the recruiter's first e-mail to an offer. Even without considering diversity, it was not an efficient process for a company that wanted to grow.

The Avvo process kept inappropriate candidates out by design. It did not find appropriate candidates, however. In machine learning parlance, the false rejection rate was too high to avoid raising the false acceptance rate. If you are trying to screen out, you miss a lot of good people. Often, biases are part of the filters. Those biases reinforced the lack of diversity.

The current process's state gave me a license to make some drastic changes. I had the support of the recruiting team and many of the managers. They all had stories of losing good candidates because of the length of the process.

Some employees and managers defended the status quo hiring process as required to maintain the quality of the development team. Luckily, there were few of them. After listening to their position and having a good discussion, I decided to move forward, knowing that I had the support of most of the group.

Removing the Coding Challenge

Many companies believe the at-home coding challenge is critical to establishing a candidate's bona fides before investing too much time in them. Many sources discuss the problems with coding challenges from a diversity perspective. The arguments against the practice that resonated with me were the following:

- Candidates often take much longer than companies expect them to complete. The Avvo guidance was that the candidate should spend no more than two hours on the challenge. One candidate estimated that he spent 12 hours on it. He wanted to make sure that he did well.
- A coding challenge is unpaid labor with no value for the results. The demand sends a message that the company places no worth on the candidates' time. I do know that some companies pay candidates a nominal fee for completing the challenge. I encourage this, but eliminating the challenge also solves this problem.

- Not all candidates have sufficient time to work on coding challenges. If a candidate is on a job search, they may get challenges from multiple companies, each with an expectation of hours of work. A candidate may already work at a stressful job or multiple jobs. They may be a caretaker to children or other relatives or have a long commute so that they can live in an affordable home. The candidate may have other issues that require their time. The challenge can be an unreasonable burden for those people.

A coding challenge requires that the candidate have the equipment and connectivity to complete the project. This requirement may not seem like an unreasonable expectation for a software developer, but not every developer may have the economic or personal safety to make this happen.

The combination of all of the above creates a bias towards people who do not have significant constraints on their time and finances. Those biases reinforce and perpetuate the lack of diversity in the industry.

As part of the hiring process, it is still critical to understand a candidate's technical maturity. We replaced the coding challenge with multiple in-person challenges during the interview loop described later in this chapter. To not overwhelm our interviewers, we focused on ensuring that the recruiter and hiring manager screens established a high culture and technical bar. This expectation on the screening required training the hiring managers on questions to ask for candidates at different levels. As we got comfortable with this process, the new screening process achieved equivalent success in identifying candidates while increasing diversity in the candidate pool and significantly decreasing the time-to-hire.[57]

The Interview Loop

There are many articles on reducing bias in the interview loop. We combined the ideas that we felt resonated the best with our culture and some of the best ideas I had experienced from prior companies.

Interviewer Training

We required that anyone participating in the interview loop participate in two training sessions:

An overall interviewer training that myself and the head of recruiting for my team presented. This training included much of the standard content of a traditional interview training effort. We added implicit bias training led by someone from Ada Developers Academy[58] (a Seattle developer training program focused on women and gender-diverse people). We had previously hired interns from Ada, and their mentors were required to take this course. It was so valuable that we made a deal with Ada to occasionally present that class at Avvo to help with our interviewer training. We also required that anyone participating in interviews became qualified on the interview questions.

A group of developers for each of the different disciplines got together to create two or three technical problems to solve, reflective of the work they did every day. Each question had a set of representative answers in a 3×3 grid. One axis represented the candidate's experience level. The other axis was unacceptable, acceptable, and excellent solutions.

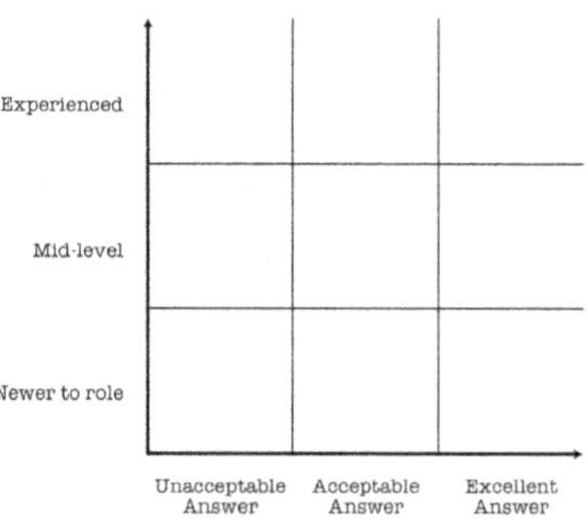

Figure 32 - The answer grid for interview questions at Avvo

We asked the same questions to any candidate regardless of the role level or their experience level. Over time, we added to the set of representative answers as we heard new answers from candidates.

To train on the question, ideally, the interviewer would attempt to answer the problem themselves. Then, they would observe a trained interviewer working with a candidate on the challenge twice. Then, a trained interviewer would watch them working with a candidate on the question themselves.

Only once the person completed all those steps could the person interview candidates. Any trained interviewer could interview for any team hiring for a role in that discipline. There was no job level required for an interviewer.

The Interviewer Panel

We ensured that at least one person from an underrepresented group was on any interviewing panel. This requirement was challenging at first. Some of the interviewers ended up having many interviews to do.

We felt it was important for two reasons. If we were interviewing someone from an underrepresented group, they would see someone like themselves and be able to ask questions (if they wanted) about their experience. If we were interviewing someone not from an underrepresented group, we would potentially catch any red flags indicating they might have challenges in a diverse environment.

This practice turned out to be very valuable.

The Interviews

As the interview training required shadowing, almost every interview would have two people from the panel. One person worked with the candidate, and one observed the discussion. This pairing meant that the hiring manager got two interpretations of what happened in the meeting and how the candidate responded to different questions. Multiple perspectives were beneficial in reducing the effect of any interviewers' biases.

We offered to let candidates bring their tools if they chose so that they could be comfortable rather than presenting the candidates with an abstract problem and having them solve it on a whiteboard or a company laptop. The interviewer and the candidate solved the technical challenges collaboratively. This approach mirrored the way that many teams at Avvo worked in a pair-programming style. The goal was to recreate, as much as possible, the actual working environment of our teams.

GAINING CREDIBILITY AS AN INCLUSIVE TECHNOLOGY EMPLOYER

Improving our interview process alone wouldn't make a significant difference if Avvo was not visible in the market as a company serious about diversity and inclusion.

The team already had multiple people volunteering at the Ada Developers Academy but had never hired an intern. We hired our first two interns from Ada in their next cohort.

We followed that by joining the new Washington Technology Industry Association Apprenti program[59] (a registered technical apprentice program focusing on underrepresented groups and veterans). We hired two apprentices from the first cohort of that program as well.

We always hired interns and apprentices in pairs to ensure they would have someone else going through a similar experience that they could use for mutual support in addition to their Avvo mentors.

Working with these programs let us partner with people deeply enmeshed in the community. We wanted to learn and listen. Working with Ada and Apprenti also introduced us to their volunteers, often experienced developers from other companies who felt strongly about increasing representation in technology.

Along with our partnership with training programs, we ensured we attended the local meetups for underrepresented groups. One of our recruiters, engineering managers, developers, or I would attend these meetups to listen and understand the challenges these groups in the industry faced. We networked as well, but only tentatively at first. We wanted to establish credibility and not just come to a single meeting and disappear.

The sustained efforts to become a part of the community taught us a lot and raised awareness of what we were trying to do at Avvo. Candidates would apply and mention the people they had already met at the company. Avvo was already hosting meetups for different technologies. Those meetings eventually became more diverse as candidates from underrepresented groups visited to see our offices.

EVOLVING THE CULTURE

The focus on increasing diversity did not have universal support. When I joined, the technology team culture was not very inclusive, and some were resistant to making any changes.

I continued to educate and discuss, but I also pushed firmly forward.

Our agile coaches and I taught new, more inclusive facilitation techniques for meetings and discussions. One of the senior managers started a mentoring program for everyone in the organization designed to support all, but especially those who might feel impostor syndrome.

Eventually, those not interested in the new culture decided to find other opportunities. In the end, this was a relatively small percentage of the team. Most were interested in being part of the new culture.

THE RESULTS

In under two years, we increased the percentage of women in the technology team from 17% to 27%. We increased the share of Black, Hispanic, and multi-racial people from 2% to 11%. Our age diversity also improved significantly. We did this while increasing the size of the team by nearly 50%. We also significantly improved our employee net promoter scores during this time.

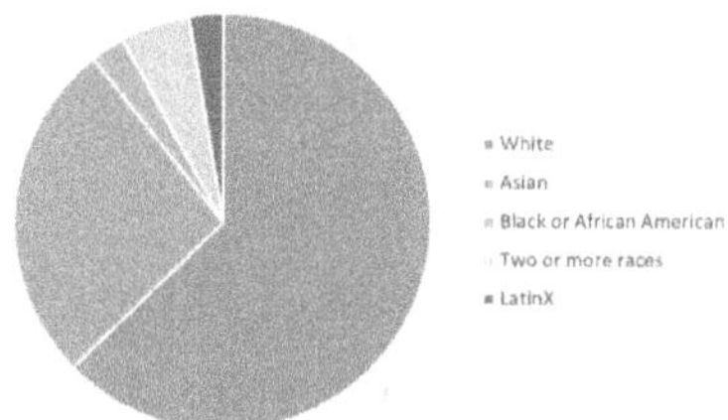

Figure 33 - Avvo Technology Team Racial Diversity in 2018

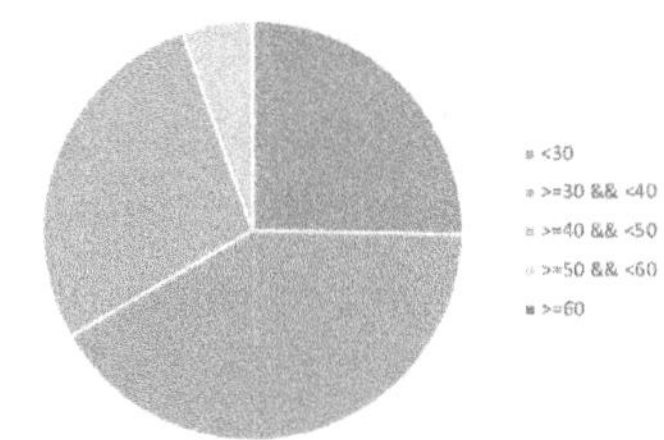

Figure 34 - Avvo Technology Team Age Diversity in 2018

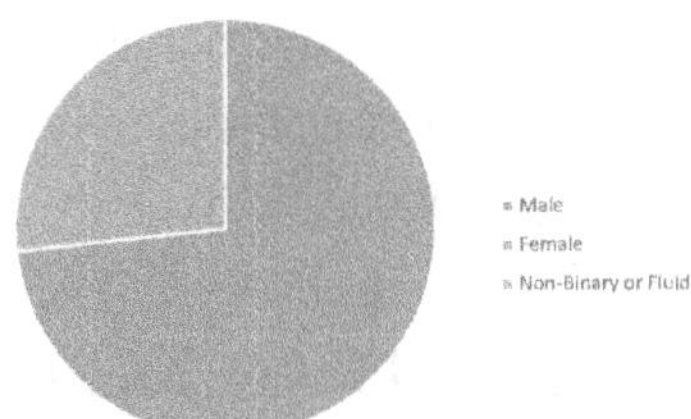

Figure 35 - Avvo Technology Team Gender Diversity in 2018

If one thing stands out to me about what we accomplished, it is a question asked by one of our developers right after our acquisition. The acquiring company's executive team hosted a town hall to answer questions from their new employees. An Avvo developer asked, "We are very proud of the diversity of our technology team at Avvo. What efforts have you put in place to make sure that your team is diverse?"

ACKNOWLEDGMENTS

There are several people mentioned in this article by title. I want to acknowledge them here as this was always a team effort and would not have succeeded without their involvement and leadership. Specifically: LaQuita Hester, a fantastic recruiter dedicated to improving diversity in the technology industry; Hunter Davis, Director of Engineering and the creator and guide for our mentoring program; Justin Weiss, Director of Engineering; and Leslie Zavisca, Engineering Manager.

Many, many others were instrumental in ways large and small. Every developer, tester, data scientist, and manager helped.

I also want to acknowledge my manager and executive team peers who had built an excellent company and supported me as I brought my team up to a level of diversity closer to what they had created. The executive team consisted of Mark Britton, Eric Dahlberg, Monica Williams, Bhavani Murugiah, Sachin Bhatia, Kelly McGill, and Jason Moss.

CHAPTER 32

Building a technical career path at Spotify

Originally published on February 8, 2016

Spotify launched a career path framework for individuals last year. Since then, I've spoken to leaders at several other companies about it. This seems to be a bit of a hot topic, so I've decided to write about our model and how we arrived at it. Hopefully, this may be useful to your company.

THE ROAD IS MORE IMPORTANT THAN THE DESTINATION

If you are trying to figure out how to approach career paths in your company, it will be tempting to take ours (or someone else's) and just use that, cargo-cult[60] style. I would highly recommend against this though. How a person matures within your company is a critical element of your company's culture. As I've written before, your culture is unique; a career path framework from another company will not build on or reinforce the values that make your company great.

WHEN SHOULD YOU CREATE A CAREER PATH FRAMEWORK?

I watched a panel on career pathing for tech startups a few years ago. One of the speakers argued that you should create a career ladder later than you think you need it, a little bit after it is really necessary. I think this is excellent advice for a few reasons. A career pathing framework is unnecessary in the early days of a company and creates a superfluous process that can be as much of a distraction as a benefit. One of the great things about the early stages of a company is that the roles people have are constantly evolving. Formalizing them too early can stunt the natural development of the organization and the individuals within it.

Eventually, as a leader, you will start hearing about people wanting to know their future at the company or how they can take on more responsibility. When this shifts from an occasional idle question to more of a groundswell, you know it is time to create something more formal.

At Spotify, we'd waited almost eight years before deciding that it was time to create a career pathing framework. The company's anti-hierarchical culture probably was a large part of the reason for not seeing this as needed. Some of the issues we had when we rolled it out were likely because we waited too long.

A few things made it clear that it was now past time to do this. There was no formal way to acknowledge career growth (via title, salary, or responsibility increases) in the individual contributor role. There was a strong belief within the organization that the way to be "promoted" was to become a Chapter Lead (line manager) or a product owner. In fact, switching to these roles at Spotify is more akin to a career change (to management or product) than it is to developing as an individual contributor.

In the spring of 2014, at a technology leadership offsite, we decided to create a "career ladder" for Spotify and quickly drew up something simple to start with. I was made the Road Manager (driver/leader) of the effort to flesh it out and then roll it out to our large organization. It seemed like a straightforward task at the time. That assumption turned out to be very naïve.

DEFINING TECHNICAL CAREER PROGRESSION, THE SPOTIFY WAY

At other companies, especially companies the size of Spotify, creating a career ladder would be something that would probably originate from the human resources organization. However, within the technology organization at Spotify, we tend to take more direct responsibility for the things that impact our culture. We feel strongly that our culture is an essential advantage in building our product. So, in Spotify Tech, we take these kinds of projects very seriously and are vocal and involved partners with our HR peers, even to the extent of driving some of these programs ourselves in partnership with HR instead of the other way around.

The goal was to create a framework that would make sense with our culture and work for employees from diverse backgrounds, in the US and Sweden, at all levels of experience, and in many different (some unique) roles. Clearly, this would require a team that could represent, as much as possible, the whole organization.

BUILDING A WORKING GROUP THAT IS REPRESENTATIVE OF THE ORGANIZATION

I put out a call to the technology organization for people who were interested in solving this challenge and who were also willing to commit the time to do it right. From the responses I received, I selected the group based on location (to maximize the number of offices represented) and on the role of the volunteer (to have a good cross-section of technology).

I also tried to get diverse opinions on the concept of career development. We had a few people who had been vocal in their skepticism of career ladders in general.[61] I wanted to make sure that those voices were present as well.

We were lucky enough to have our Chief Human Resources Officer (CHRO) join for several of the early meetings. Naturally, our HR Business Partners for technology were also involved. Their domain expertise was critical throughout the process.

DOING IT RIGHT TAKES A LOT LONGER THAN YOU'D EXPECT

At first, I thought that a few months of twice-a-week meetings would be sufficient to conceive and launch the program. That turned out to be ridiculously optimistic. We were able to largely define the framework in a few months, but to create something like this, in an organic, bottom-up manner, for a large organization, requires many cycles of feedback gathering and incorporation. In the end, it took nearly six months from the beginning of the working group to the official Request For Comment (RFC) document. It is now over 18 months since that initial working group meeting, and it still feels like we're getting used to having the program in place, even as we prepare for the second iteration. We have spent a lot of the last year supporting the rollout and adoption of the framework.

SOME GUIDING PRINCIPLES

The working group began as you might expect, talking about the aspirations for the effort and comparing our own past experiences with career ladders at other companies. We talked about which of those elements made sense in Spotify's culture. Quickly, we realized that the simple career ladder proposed by the tech leadership group wouldn't make sense. Within the first or second meeting, that proposal was officially dead, and we started from scratch.

We agreed on a few principles early on:

- This would not be a "ladder" with an up-or-out mentality. We wanted to support people who wished to maintain their current level of responsibility.
- The basis for advancement was a demonstration of behaviors and not achievements. We wanted our framework to be a true model of professional development. It should be about who you are, and not about what you've done. In a failure-safe environment like Spotify, we didn't want to penalize people for taking big chances.
- We wanted to support changing roles without punishing people for developing themselves. In other career ladders we'd seen, the role becomes a silo. Switching roles could mean a literal demotion since the requirements of a level are tied to specific areas of achievement in a specific role.
- We wanted this framework to reflect our team-oriented and autonomy-driven culture. Teamwork is critical to our way of working, and we wanted to ensure this was part of personal development.
- We wanted to support both generalists and specialists. Many folks at Spotify move around the organization to develop a breadth of skills, while others like to get especially deep in specific technology areas. We wanted to support both of these types of people.
- We believed that career progression is marked by your impact on progressively larger areas of the organization, your sphere of influence.

We shunned the word ladder from the start, influenced in part by our career ladder skeptics and our desire to support multiple ways of development. Struggling to describe our career pathing model, we eventually came upon the word "steps," thinking more about rocks in a stream than a staircase. The rocks would let you move side to side, or even backward, to move forward eventually. The framework was named Spotify Career Steps.

A SET OF FIVE CHARACTERISTICS

We were able to build on some of the efforts that had come before in the technology organization. Specifically, the Agile Coaches guild had spent time developing a common set of core capabilities they thought each Spotify developer should have. This became the basis for the areas of development of our framework. We then added two additional areas to reflect professional development within our culture.

The five characteristics of Spotify employees that we identified were:

- Values team success over individual success
- Continuously improves themselves and their team
- Holds themselves and others accountable
- Thinks about the business impact of their work
- Demonstrates mastery of their discipline

I will go further into these characteristics in the next chapter.

A SET OF FOUR STEPS

There was some discussion around the number of "levels" to have. We decided it was easier to add more levels later than remove them if we created too many. Given that we had already decided that being more senior meant being a resource for larger and larger parts of the organization, mapping "levels" to our levels of organization seemed like a reasonable first approach.

The four steps of career development at Spotify that we decided on were:

- **Individual** – at this level, you are new to working and are figuring out how to be a productive and contributing member of the company.
- **Squad / Chapter** (these are the teams that people primarily belong to) – you are now a contributing member of a team and are a resource for the people you work with every day.
- **Tribe / Guild** (these are the larger teams organizationally or functionality that people are part of) – Now, you are a resource beyond your immediate team. Either because you have depth in a technology (and help others or other teams around that technology), you are skilled at solving difficult problems that span teams, or you can be counted on to lead other developers in your tribe to solve large cross-squad problems.
- **Technology / Company** (the highest levels of the organization) – The developers at this level are resources for the entire company based on their technical and leadership skills. They are expected to spend a significant amount of

their time working across the organization.

A MAP OF CAREER GROWTH AT SPOTIFY

The five characteristics and four steps created a map of professional development at Spotify. We then spent significant amounts of time defining each step's characteristics.

One decision we made that I think was especially good was that mastery was only one of the five characteristics. That is the only area where we differentiate based on role (since mastery as a coach is significantly different than mastery as a mobile developer). This also helped reinforce that switching roles didn't necessarily mean moving backward in your career development, as most of the characteristics were universal.

Much of the focus of the feedback we got was on the content of this map. This makes sense because this was where the model became concrete for people. We were defining what would be expected of employees in technology, after all.

A GROUP EDITING PROCESS

We settled into a rhythm of working in a shared Google document, mob editing. Non-pair changes followed our code review guidelines: an edit was made in the doc as a suggestion, and two separate approval comments to the proposal were needed to accept the change.

The current version of the document (we would "fork" or create a new copy regularly) was then shared with progressively larger groups of managers and employees to get their feedback. Their comments and suggestions were then incorporated, after which a new version would be shared.

The rounds of feedback and tweaking were extremely valuable. We realized we weren't doing enough to support introverts in the initial versions, for example, and had to go back and make significant changes.

After several months of revisions and sharing with progressively larger groups, we finally created an official RFC version, which was then shared with the entire organization for comments and suggestions.

This particular collaborative editing and progressive review process ended up working quite well. There were some improvements that I will recommend in the third part of this series.

At this time, I want to recognize the initial working group that was instrumental in creating the process and the document. We worked so well as a group that, in retrospect, it was hard to remember whose ideas were whose. Any suggestion that any of us had was improved by the others involved. While I am writing about what we did, the work itself was a truly collective effort by Chris Angove, Daniel Prata, David Poblador I Garcia, Eli Daniel, Henrique Imbertti, Jessica Joelsson, Kevin Goldsmith, Kinshuk Mishra, Olof Svedström, and Will Meyer.

CHAPTER 33

Spotify Technology Career Steps

Originally published on February 15, 2016

This chapter contains the actual first version of the Technical Career Steps as published within Spotify.

MOTIVATION BEHIND THE STEPS FRAMEWORK

As Technology within Spotify has grown over the years we have learned that people striving to increase their impact often wanted to become a Chapter Lead or Product Owner even if they might have preferred the role of an individual contributor engineer. Everyone in Spotify Tech should have a way to grow their careers and expand the impact of their -work no matter what role they play. A shift into a Chapter Lead or PO position is not necessary.

The Steps Framework provides a way to do this.

THE STEPS FRAMEWORK

As your career evolves within Spotify, you will likely take on a variety of roles, in a variety of contexts. You will work with multiple teams, on multiple projects, perhaps in very different domains or perhaps in a smaller area of specialty. You will build capabilities and mastery. Your impact on Spotify will grow, and so likely will your sphere of influence.

Your career development within Technology will therefore be a journey — sometimes sideways, sometimes forwards, and always flexible. There are some common patterns in the series of roles people decide to take on, and in which disciplines and expertise areas they focus, but this is not rigidly defined. It is up to you, with the help of your manager, to choose a path that aligns your interests and the company's, and that helps you develop, grow, and meet your own unique personal goals.

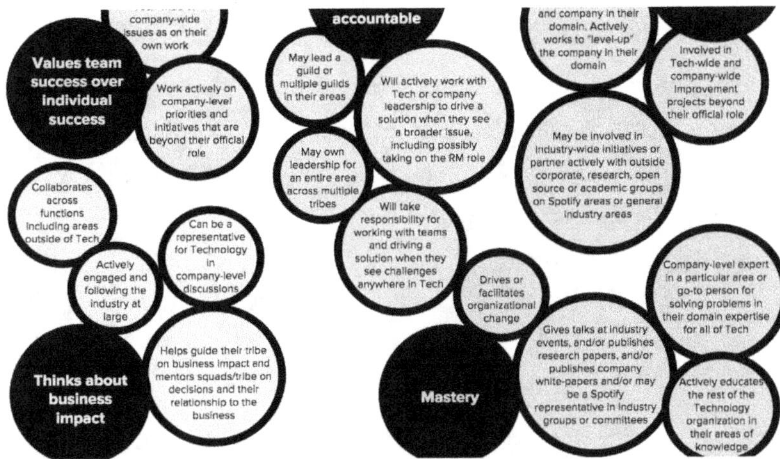

Figure 36 - The Career Steps Framework

Throughout this journey, as you gain experience and develop your skills, you will have greater and greater impact. In other words, the degree to which you contribute to the success of Spotify — its team and its mission — will grow over time.

The Steps Framework is designed to provide you with:

- The opportunity to explore new roles, skills, contexts and disciplines over time, avoiding a specific, rigidly-defined "track"
- A way to understand your progression toward greater and greater impact, independent of specific role or discipline
- A set of well-defined expectations corresponding to defined points in this progression

In Practice: Disciplines, Roles & Steps

In practical terms, supporting this development journey requires a more complex framework than a typical vertically-oriented hierarchy or "career ladder". There are three key elements in the Steps Framework:

- A **Discipline** is a domain of expertise and impact. Examples include:
  - coaching
  - software development
  - testing
  - project management
- A **Role** is a way in which you engage with a team, a project, or a discipline. They are not all formally defined, but there are some common ones. Examples include:
  - software engineer
  - tester
  - road manager
  - technical product owner
  - chapter lead
  - agile coach
- A **Step** is the combination of a well-defined set of expectations and behaviors associated with a particular degree of impact on Spotify. As you take Steps on your career path, your impact grows.

In the end, your path will involve taking *Steps* forward, growing your impact and broadening your influence while you evolve through specific *Roles* in various *Disciplines*. Your compensation is influenced by your Step, aligning your performance to the positive impact you are able to have on your team, your product, and Spotify as a whole.

Moving to a new Step in a given domain represents both an acknowledgment of what you have done and a commitment from your manager that you will get bigger challenges in the future.

Your Step is a measure of your personal growth and is intended for use in discussions about career development between you and your manager. Your Step is private: only you and your manager can see your Step. But we believe in transparency, and so will re-evaluate whether everyone's Step should be public in some form after we have lived with the framework for a while. It is much easier to share this information later than to un-share it if it becomes problematic.

Behaviors and our expectations at different Steps

We have identified five sets of behaviors that provide a framework for understanding and talking about the expectations on all of us, at different levels of impact. They are:

- Values team success over individual success
- Continuously improves themselves and team
- Holds themselves and others accountable
- Thinks about the business impact of their work
- Demonstrates mastery of their discipline

The greater the impact, the more we expect in each of these areas. A "senior" technologist who's helping to set company-wide strategy will need to make these values manifest in different (and more sophisticated) ways than a fresh-out-of-school member of a squad.

The path

There is no one path through this framework. It is up to you and your manager to navigate the set of roles and the contexts in which those roles can be played, finding good ways to align your interests and your organization's needs. Through this process, you will always learn and grow, increasing your impact on the company, and thus moving to different Steps. There is no expected amount of time that you will spend on each Step. Some people will move through them faster, and some will go slower. Some will reach a Step and choose not push towards the next Step, instead growing in other ways. The steps themselves are a measure of professional maturity and are therefore cumulative. A Tribe/Guild-step contributor shows all the behaviors of the Individual-, Squad/Chapter- and Tribe/Guild-steps.

CAREER STEPS FOR TECH EMPLOYEES

There are five characteristics that every individual in Tech should develop as part of their professional growth at Spotify:

- **Values team success over individual success:** We are a team and not a collection of unaffiliated individuals. You may be part of several teams: your squad, your chapter, your guild(s), your tribe. Contributing to the success of each of these groups is more beneficial to the company, the product, and our customers than chasing your own success at the cost of your teams.
- **Continuously improves (self and team):** Spotify believes in never settling for the status quo. We are always focused on learning and growing.
- **Holds themselves and others accountable:** As a company we value transparency and autonomy. These values must be coupled with accountability if we are to succeed. Taking responsibility for your own actions and the actions of the team and holding others to this standard is critical for us to be able to trust and work with each other.
- **Thinks about business impact:** Spotify is a business. If we wish to keep working within this culture that we've built, we need to make sure that we are aligned with that business. Understanding how the choices you make affect the company is important for your growth as a professional.
- **Mastery:** While the other characteristics talk about expectations and behaviors that are independent of your domain or role, mastery is specifically about becoming a better software engineer, agile coach, technical product owner, QE, QA or TA. There are items marked for each of these disciplines. Anything that isn't marked is expected of all roles.

We have also identified four Steps in your career path at Spotify. Each Step is marked not only by increased responsibility, but also by your increased impact within tech.

- **Individual Step.** At this step, you are focused primarily on being a useful contributor, gaining experience and learning how to be effective on their team. It is not expected that a member of technology would remain at this step during their entire time at Spotify. At this step, your focus should be on growing so that you can support your team. This is the only step where there is an expectation that all members of technology should move toward the next step.

- **Squad/Chapter Step.** At this step, you are a resource for your chapter or your squad, either as a domain specialist for your team, or as a generalist/problem solver for them. You should be able to lead smaller efforts coordinating with other members of your team and drive them to completion and/or dig into tough problems and solve them independently taking in feedback from your peers and focusing on the outcome.

- **Tribe/Guild Step.** At this step, you have an impact across squads or chapters. You are a resource for a larger group as a domain expert or generalist. You will lead cross-team (squad/tribe/chapter) efforts involving more people and drive them to completion and/or you will take on large challenges, working with diverse stakeholders in multiple teams to solve a problem that affects your larger organization.

- **Technology/Company Step.** At this step, your focus is significantly on supporting Tech-wide or company-wide initiatives. You will Road Manage projects that span tribes and be responsible for solving Tech-wide problems, and/or you will also represent Tech in company and/or industry forums, and/or you will be a go-to person across the company to solve very complex problems

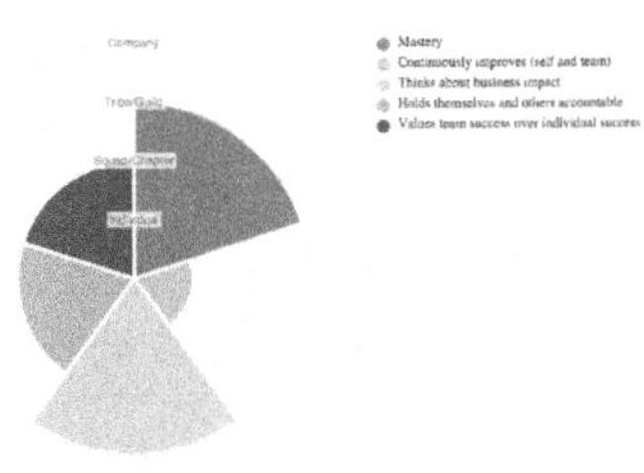

**Figure 37 - Sample Spider Graph of
Spotify Competency Areas**

On recognition and promotions

When you are consistently demonstrating the behaviors and sustained impact of someone at a wider Step, your manager should recommend you for an official promotion (as long as you are willing to accept the increased expectations going forward).

The process for promotion depends on the Step involved:

- A chapter lead can promote one of their individual step employees to squad/chapter step without outside approval, though the chapter lead will make this decision in part based on feedback from that employee's peers in the squad and chapter.

- Promotions from squad/chapter step to tribe/guild step must be approved by the relevant tribe lead, after consultation with tribe-level leadership.
- Promotions to technology/company step must be approved by the CTO, after consultation with technical leadership, including people currently at the technology/company step.

Since we place so much value at Spotify on being an effective member of a team; promotion to the next step, at all levels, should involve consultation with a varied group of the person's peers. This can be done using the loops performance review tool in addition to direct conversation, for example.

Formal promotion to a new Step will normally come with an immediate compensation increase, as well as an immediately increased scope of responsibilities. The promotion represents a commitment from both sides: you will keep executing at the more advanced level, and your manager will continue to provide opportunities to have broader impact.

Examples of broader responsibilities as part of being at a more senior step for a developer could include things like:

- driving the technical implementation of a new feature for a squad at the squad/chapter step
- figuring out how a tribe should adapt their systems for anonymization at the tribe/guild step
- leading the CDN technology strategy for content delivery, including technical feasibility, cost/benefit analysis, and vendor selection at the technology/company step

Public recognition will frequently be decoupled from formal promotion. We believe it's more effective to recognize people for successful completion of important projects than for reaching a (somewhat rare) career milestone. So we expect to see more announcements like "Please join me in congratulating Jane Jones, who drove this project to completion over the last few months" and fewer announcements like "Please join me in congratulating Jane Jones, who has officially been promoted to the Tribe/Guild Step".

On Setting the Step for a New Employee

It can be hard to tell what step a new employee is on based solely on their interviews. To give the employee time to acclimate to Spotify and their role, their official step will not be determined until their six-month review. During that review, the step is set through a discussion between the new employee and their manager.

The new employee should do a self-evaluation with the framework to see how much they believe each behavior represents them. The manager should talk to the peers of the employee and use their own knowledge and experience from working with the employee to do an initial evaluation of how the different behaviors in the framework describe the employee. A discussion between the manager and the employee will show where they agree and where they differ, and allow them to reach a decision on which behaviors describe the employee today. This also sets the context of areas to focus on in the near future for growth.

On Compensation

Your compensation as a Spotify Employee within Technology is influenced by the Steps Framework: having a bigger impact on the company should lead to higher pay in a straightforward and transparent way.

We want to make sure Spotify salaries are following the market. Therefore we get salary benchmarks from specialised suppliers and industry leaders in this area. Since the salary benchmarks are used as a recommendation and not as strict guidelines when setting salaries we will not share them internally. We've always used market data to help guide our pay principles. Since H2 of 2015 we are matching them to work within our steps framework.

The salary benchmarks for Steps overlap each other. This means that a person at the Individual Step can earn as much as someone at the Squad/Chapter Step and vice versa.

On Titles

Steps do not map to titles. We approach titles differently depending on whether we're talking about internal or external use.

Internally:

- Scopes of impact have defined names — the Individual Step -> Technology/Company Step.
- Roles have defined names — some more formally defined than others.
- Roles are typically more useful for internal communications than anything else.

Externally:

- Employees have a tremendous amount of flexibility regarding how they represent themselves externally.
- They can use their roles, they can use more standard titles that they feel are more communicable.
- We may in the future provide examples of external titles that commonly map to our internal role names to facilitate this.
- We expect employees and their managers to work together to come up with appropriate external title usage.

Expectations for each Step

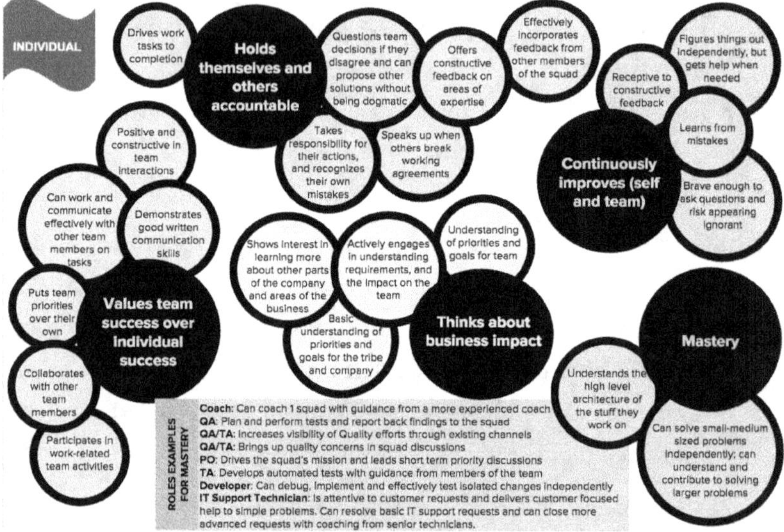

Figure 38 - Individual Step

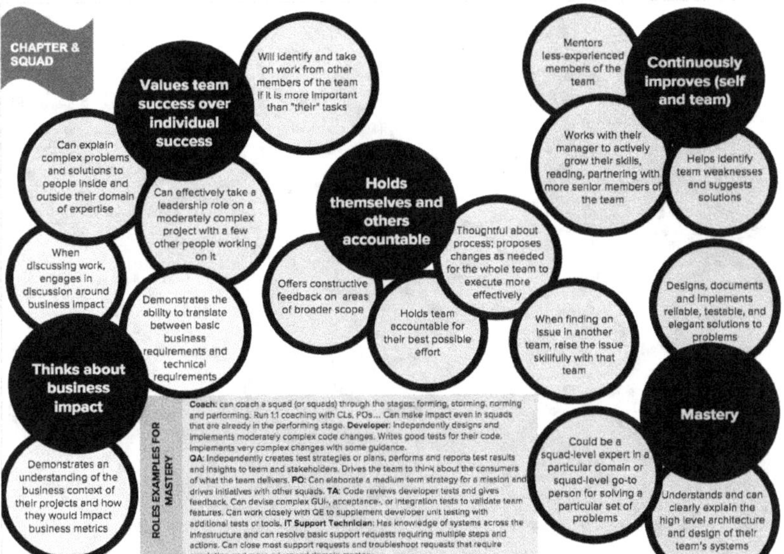

Figure 39 - Squad Step

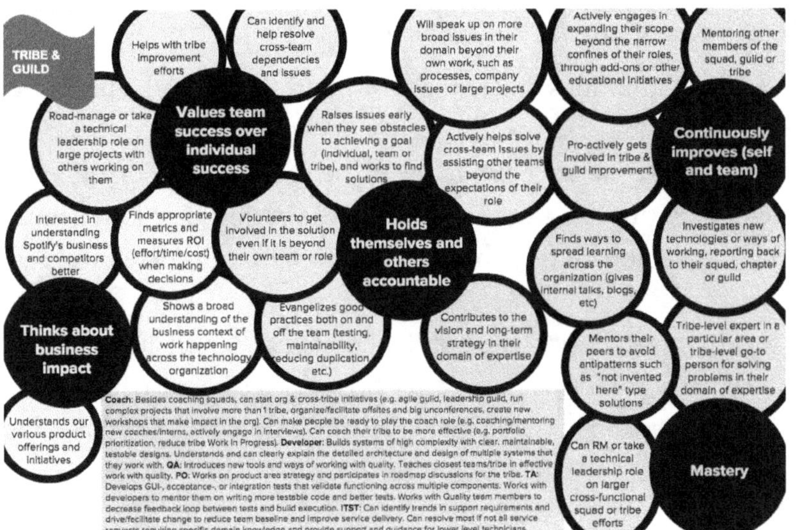

Figure 40 - Tribe Step

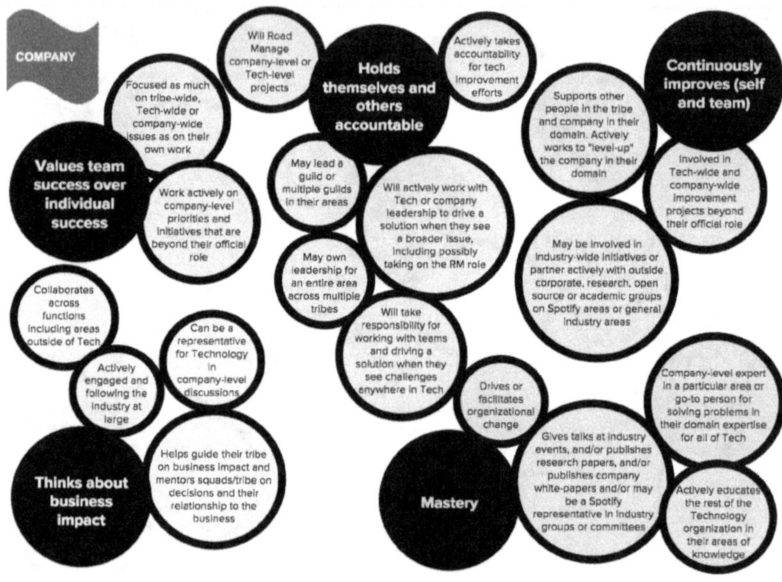

Figure 41 – Company Step

On Requirements vs. Examples

A few questions are common around the examples provided in the framework: are the behaviors in the bubble diagrams hard requirements? How many of behaviors must someone be demonstrating, and how consistently, and for how long *must they be demonstrating them before they are considered to be at a particular step?

The most important point is that managerial judgment is always required: this framework provides a structure for fostering conversation between managers and employees, but it cannot ever provide a detailed recipe for how to handle any particular situation. So the answers are intentionally not black-and-white.

The intention of the Steps Framework is to describe what it looks like for an individual to have increasing levels of impact on the Spotify tech organization. But the truth is that there are lots of ways to have big impact, and we want to support all of them. Someone might be moving the whole company forward through their deep expertise in a particular technology, and by putting on their headphones in a corner and singlehandedly writing a huge and critical piece of infrastructure that accelerates the work of hundreds of other people. Someone else might move the the whole company forward by spending lots of time in meetings, driving consensus and resolving conflict as the company does something new. These, and lots of variants in between, are all valuable.

So the answer is that the behaviors in the bubbles are mostly examples: many of the bubbles describe a specific activity more than a general behavior. These "activities" are mostly meant as examples of step-appropriate behaviors, as opposed to specific activities required to demonstrate that behavior. In aggregate, they paint a picture of what we mean when we say "tribe and guild impact", "squad and chapter impact", etc. But they should be treated as triggers for discussion rather than a checklist. Are you doing this thing? Would your work have more impact if you did? In general, we think these are all valuable things that people in tech should do. But it's not about seeing a behavior once and checking it off, or seeing a behavior consistently and checking it off, or about checking off 80% of the bubbles at some level or 100% of the bubbles. It's about the impact that your work has over time, and these bubbles are a loose proxy.

FREQUENTLY ASKED QUESTIONS

What about my special situation?

These guidelines should never trump common sense. People are complicated, and there may be some special cases that this framework does not address well. Managerial judgement will always be needed, in all cases.

I do not see myself as a developer, QA, TPO or a coach. My discipline is not mentioned in the framework, what expectations are set on me?

The framework provides examples for four of the most common disciplines within tech, but there are others. It would not be possible to define good examples for all possible disciplines or combinations of these. The existing examples should inspire and help you and your manager to set the expectations for you even if the names of the disciplines are not a perfect match. If a tribe after evaluating the framework later comes to the conclusion that the present disciplines are not helpful enough and need arises to define new examples for other disciplines they can introduce new ones.

Is there a set of formally-defined roles?

No. As context and ways of working differ across Technology, formal, pre-defined roles would not fit into a lot of squads. We do have disciplines (e.g. coaching, software development, tool-smithing, quality assisting, …) to guide skill sets and expectations, but as an individual contributor in Tech we do not forcefully limit our work to one of these.

What is the connection between Roles and Steps? Do I have to be at a specific Step to take on certain Roles?

Not for most roles – but some. Examples: You won't be a good chapter lead if your sphere of influence is Individual, hence being squad/chapter step or above is needed. To be a Chief Architect your sphere of influence needs to be on a company level.

Is this a reporting hierarchy?

Reporting is based on your Role and Discipline, and not your Step. Based on their role, a Software engineer of any step can still report to a Chapter Lead.

Are Steps like "Senior"/etc. designations?

Steps are a tool to facilitate career development and do not confer any title.

Do I have to demonstrate the behaviors in all value areas to be considered for a wider Step?

As a rule, yes. Steps are intended to reflect growing spheres of influence and impact. We believe all the competencies listed are necessary for someone to really have the increased level of impact that a new Step represents. However, people are complicated, and there may be cases where someone's strength in one area compensates for a weakness in another.

Do I need to continuously move through steps during my career at Spotify?

This is something to discuss with your manager. While we expect engineers to continuously improve their skills there is no rule that one must also continuously increase their sphere of influence. Individual step is considered an introductory step for an inexperienced contributor. We do expect that employees will move from the individual step as they become contributing members of their squad.

What happens if I want to move to a step with less impact?

You may choose to embrace a new discipline where you have a significantly lower level of mastery. There may be other situations that lead you toward this choice. Again people are complicated and we neither can or should try to anticipate every situation. If you decide that you want to make this kind of change, discuss it with your manager. Note that your compensation is tied with your Step.

How does this relate to loops?

Loops (Spotify's performance review framework) is a tool focused on performance development that puts employees in the driving seat. It can be very useful for your career evolution. Promotions are a separate process from Loops.

How does this relate to Priorities and Achievements?

Priorities and Achievements are a way for you to make commitments to goals and measure your performance against them. This can help determine your salary adjustments within your range year to year, but it is not tied to your step which will determine your salary range itself. As you increase your impact by moving to wider steps, your priorities and achievements should reflect that.

When can I get promoted?

When you and your manager agree that you are consistently operating at the next Step. Specifically, promotions do not need to be tied to the annual salary review cycle. See "On Recognitions and Promotions" for the details on how the promotion process works.

To what extent is this a tool, guidance, or a formal policy?

This framework is intended to provide a concrete toolset for employees and their managers. It is the model all of Technology is using. While deviations may make sense and be needed in some cases, that is the exception and is something that should be discussed at the tribe leadership level.

How does my Career Step affect my salary?

Your career step is used to determine a range of pay based on people at a similar sphere of impact in similar disciplines. This pay range gives guidance to managers on competitive rates of pay in the industry. It does not set your salary from year to year. Your pay change set in your yearly salary review is based on your performance based on expectations during the previous year.

Do I need to be promoted to increase my salary?

No. You can stay at a step and continue to increase your salary year over year. The salary ranges from step to step overlap significantly and they track the market (which is evaluated every year). Your salary increase is based on your performance, your behaviors, and the market.

How do I as an introvert fulfill the expectations on communication and networking in this framework? It seems to be tailored for more extroverted people.

The important thing is to make a positive impact. Given that, you have to find your own way, something that you feel comfortable with. Some people prefer the written language, others the vocal one. Some people share their ideas right away, others prefer to take time to think and elaborate. You just need to make sure you are communicating in an effective and constructive manner.

CHAPTER 34

Things We Learned Creating Technology Career Steps

Originally published on February 22, 2016

THE LAUNCH TO THE ORGANIZATION

We launched the request for comments (RFC) version of Career Steps at a special town hall for Spotify's entire technology department in December 2014. Leading up to the town hall, we'd done several reviews of earlier iterations with increasingly larger groups from the organization, and we'd given training in Steps and conversations around Steps for every manager in Technology. We left plenty of time for questions in the presentation, which was good. We prompted people to read the document, ask questions in the document, via a mailing list or a Slack channel that we set up, or ask their manager. In retrospect, we should have followed up with some more opportunities to talk to our working group face-to-face. Most of the organization would have been reading the document for the first time after the town hall, and some had only read earlier drafts.

The Relationship between Steps and Compensation

One area was still incomplete when we launched Steps, and this incompleteness was an issue that challenged us for a long time. The vague area was the connection between your step and your salary. We had asserted that there was a connection, but when we launched the framework, our Compensation and Benefits team had not finished reviewing how this should work. We knew the generalities but not the details. This lack of clarity left us in a very challenging situation since we had given Steps a critical connection to the individuals in the organization, but we couldn't yet explain it. We knew that there needed to be a connection between Steps and compensation. Suppose we were saying that Steps embodied what we valued from the members of our organization, but the salary of those members was determined entirely separately. In that case, we essentially contradicted ourselves and undercut the framework's effectiveness.

The lack of clarity around compensation created tension in adopting Steps with some individuals in the organization. Unfortunately, the connection between salary and step wasn't resolved until nearly a year later. This meant that the first salary review after launching Steps couldn't use the framework. This was a failure on one level, but it was also positive in some ways. Since Steps were very new, having people get a step and immediately have it affect their salary might have led to many bad feelings; by delaying the tie to compensation, people had time to adjust to the system and potentially change their step before their first salary review.

Our inability to talk concretely about Steps and salary also created misperceptions about how this would work. We had to spend much effort working through these only to have them reappear in mail threads and discussions repeatedly. The most persistent misperception was that the only way to change your salary was by changing your step. This naturally caused much concern that was difficult to dispel until the Compensation and Benefits team had completed their work. Our C&B team did a stellar job of creating a fair and very progressive system that allowed good overlap in salary ranges between the steps and a lot of headroom. Since that has been completed, we hopefully have put many of the concerns to rest, especially as we are now using Steps as part of our current salary review.

Behavior Versus Achievements

We made an explicit decision around Career Steps that your behaviors, not your achievements, characterized career growth. This is counter to the way career advancement works at many other companies. It was something that we not only felt strongly about; it was something that we were proud of. In a culture that encourages innovation, failure (and learning from failure) is a natural occurrence. If we only rewarded success, we were punishing failure and discouraging risk-taking. We also wanted to encourage real personal growth and not a culture of checking off achievements on a list and expecting a promotion. This naturally created some ambiguity around the requirements for each step. The working group embraced this ambiguity as a way of giving managers some room to make decisions and also to encourage discussion between the individual and their manager.

In retrospect, our approach was a bit naive in a few ways. While we, as an organization, are very comfortable with ambiguity in many areas, recognizing a person's career advancement was personal and had personal consequences. Some individuals were very uncomfortable with this ambiguity and would have preferred more concrete requirements around promotion. Another group thought even the examples given were too much of a checklist. This is still something that we are working through.

We seek ways to support those in the organization who want more clarity without being too prescriptive. We have discussed creating lists of (anonymized) examples of the behaviors. The concern is that this would lead to people treating the examples as achievements to be checked off instead.

This has been a particularly thorny path to traverse with some very vocal minorities, but most of the organization seems to have understood the concept.

Having Greater Impact Means Not Working on a Team?

There was one aspect of the Steps Framework that we hadn't anticipated being controversial and didn't come up often in our earlier reviews of the document. This was the aspect of Steps being a reflection of your sphere of influence. The core idea around this was that as you increase your professional maturity, you will naturally become a resource for ever more extensive parts of the organization, either through your technical leadership, deep technical skills, or general problem-solving ability. This increasing sphere of influence brings new, broader responsibilities with it. This aligned well with our experiences in the working group at Spotify and other companies. For some individuals, the idea that they couldn't move to a Tribe/Guild step without working outside their squads was a concern.

At Spotify, we point to the squad as the central place where work gets done. It is at the top of our inverted servant-leadership hierarchy. The question we repeatedly heard was: Why couldn't someone just be better at what they do and get "promoted" for doing the same role if they were adding value to their team? I think this was a case where we could have presented the reasoning for this decision in a better way in the document.

Not Enough Chances for Advancement?

When deciding on the number of steps to create, we decided to keep the number relatively small. The thought was that it was easier to add more than it was to remove some. Four steps are not many changes in a potentially forty-plus-year career. The expectation was that people would potentially stay at a step for a very long time. This was very discouraging for some people who felt that they would never be "promoted" in their Spotify career.

Here, we missed the understanding that a segment of our organization wanted the opportunity for recognition of increasing advancement. We had not been doing this before in any respect, so we hadn't considered that it was something that a group desired. We were wrong about that, and with Steps, we weren't giving that group enough opportunity to get it. This problem was a significant oversight since we knew that part of what encouraged people to make career changes to management or the product team was this lack of recognition. As a result, recognition is an active discussion area for successive iterations of the framework.

ASSIGNING STEPS

After the town hall presentation introducing Steps, we gave people some time to respond to the RFC version of the document and feedback to the working group. In January, we started the process of making sure every individual contributor in the technology organization had a step. Initially, we left the process up to each tribe. This was a mistake. The tribes needed more guidance on how to make this process work. Luckily, at Spotify, we are quite good at figuring these things out and sharing good ideas. The Infrastructure and Operations Tribe came up with the suggestion that each individual should use the Steps document to make a self-assessment of which step they should be on, then have a discussion with their manager about where they agreed and disagreed. This was quickly adopted as a good process across most of the organization.

Once every chapter lead completed these discussions within each tribe, the tribe would meet to ensure that each manager was assigning steps to their employees similarly. Functional managers in different parts of the organization also met to do a similar exercise. These synchronizations helped ensure we were fair and consistent across the entire organization. Before the steps for individuals were finalized, the Tribe Leads and CTO met to go over all the recommendations for the Tribe/Guild and Tech/Company steps. This served two very valuable purposes. It assured consistency across the entire organization for the individuals on these steps. It also made the senior technical leadership aware of who these individuals were and what their managers thought they contributed to the organization.

The process of assigning steps to individuals was completed in March, but we also had a problem here. Adding steps into our HR systems was a more significant challenge than our HRIS team had anticipated. So, the steps were assigned in the spring but weren't readily visible to employees, their managers, or HR until the fall. This also meant we had difficulties tracking which teams were behind in submitting steps for their employees. We couldn't quickly run reports to see how steps were distributed as well.

Once we finally worked it out, we found we were missing a lot of data. Some employees had never been assigned a step. Some employees had transitioned between teams or roles, and their step hadn't been communicated. Steps hadn't been integrated into the onboarding process, so many new employees had never gotten their step. There were a bunch of other issues as well. These had to be rectified before we could do our salary review. The lack of visibility also contributed to an "out of sight, out of mind" issue where some people or managers didn't do much with the framework after the initial discussion.

In retrospect, the working group should have taken ownership of this until the issues with the HR system were handled. Unfortunately, there was some poor communication around the timeline for the fixes, and we thought that the problem was solved.

POSITIVE RESULTS

Once the Steps Framework was launched, we started getting strong positive feedback from the organization in addition to the concerns noted above. Many of our line managers (Chapter Leads) were previously individual contributors; they especially appreciated having a structure to help frame personal development discussions. Also, many individuals told us how it was good to have some structure and understanding about how to grow at Spotify. The working group collected feedback in multiple ways, including interviewing employees in different offices.

We wanted to have some real data in addition to our anecdotal evidence to have greater confidence that we were adding value. Some robust supporting data came from our yearly Great Place to Work survey, where in the Technology Organization, the "Management makes its expectations clear" measurement increased by four percentage points year over year, and the "I am offered training or development to further myself professionally" measurement increased by six percentage points. Several things could have impacted these measurements, but we had a reasonable belief that Steps had a part in these increases.

While we had started our effort with the desire to be data-driven, as we went to measure our impact, it was clear that we were not as rigorous as we should have been. We should have started the entire effort with some qualitative numbers on how the organization felt about the support they had for personal development driven by a survey or poll. This would have given us better metrics to measure ourselves against and would help us guide future iterations. This is something that the working group is actively pursuing.

LOSS OF FOCUS

Once the steps were assigned, the working group started moving into a less active phase. There was a strong sense of accomplishment but also weariness. From meeting twice a week and working on the document in between the meetings, meeting with individuals and teams to discuss steps, training the managers, launching the effort, and supporting the initial rollout, there had been a tremendous amount of work done. However, this wasn't anyone's main job; we were all moonlighting to do this. Also, during this time, many of us were involved in a large project demanding our focus. It felt like we had completed our mission, and it was time to move on to new things. Unfortunately, we were wrong.

In this post-launch phase, we made some of our biggest mistakes. We'd launched the framework, but our support for it was largely put on hold. We hadn't established the necessary structures to train new employees in Steps. We stopped sending updates and communicating about what was happening around Steps. This led to many questions and confusion in the organization around what was going on with the effort.

Eventually, we realized our error. At that point, we had to do some cleanup and rebuilding work to get the program back on track. Luckily, the HRIS team had done their thing during this time, as had Comp and Benefits. We also had our first Steps-enabled salary review to do. We were also very fortunate that parts of the organization had started to embrace Steps and were using it in several ways to support individual growth through structured training and formal or informal mentoring. These other efforts helped keep Steps from being forgotten by the technology team.

The working group had been inactive too long at this point. Most of the members had new commitments. For a time, we continued moving the effort forward with the participation we had, but it was clear that we needed to move into a new phase, which would require a new group.

CURRENT STATUS

Currently, the Working Group is reforming with new members. The current members are engaged with our Human Resources team on training in Steps for Managers and Employees. We've also started working on the next iteration of Steps, addressing some lessons learned and feedback received now that Technology has been living with the framework for a while. The new group will have a few members from the first version, which will give some continuity to the effort and provide some history, but the rest of the group will be new, which should inject some new ideas and approaches to the work.

The leadership of the technology organization has been doing a lot to support the framework. We are actively giving more responsibility and opportunities to our Tribe/Guild step employees, and we are also looking to grow our Squad/Chapter step employees to the next step if that interests them.

We've had several promotions between steps during the year, which is a serious measure of validation. That would be a significant issue if people weren't moving between steps.

Additionally, in my organization, two managers who were also highly skilled technologists moved back to being individual contributors. They were excited by the possibility of being technical leaders without being people managers.

Many tribes are now considering their Tribe/Guild step people as incremental members of their squads so that when they are helping outside their squad, they don't adversely affect the ability of the squad to get its work done.

LESSONS

We learned many lessons in the creation of Steps. If there was one thing that I think was paramount, it was that this ended up being a lot more like Culture Change than we expected it to be. We thought we were creating something to support and reinforce our company culture. In fact, we were specifying something where there had been only people's conceptions before. So, while we feel that we did create something generally well-aligned and supportive of the Spotify culture, it was still a change for many individuals in the organization. If we had realized that, we would have treated the rollout more like a Culture Change effort and used more of those techniques in our rollout plans.

Another major lesson I didn't capture above was that we didn't have our long-term support plan in place. We did put together a plan around supporting the effort, but we created that plan after the launch of Steps. As mentioned above, the working group was tired from getting the framework to that point. It would have been much better to think through the long-term support needs of the work closer to the beginning of the effort and then adjust them later as we learned more.

I think that the process of using increasingly large groups to give feedback was quite good. It resulted in a much better outcome than if we had just generated the framework in a smaller, more isolated group. However, we primarily used the organization's managers and leadership to collect feedback. We would have benefited from including groups of individual contributors, especially if we could include the same people in multiple reviews of the document, just as we did with the coaches and leadership.

Once the Steps Framework was starting to solidify, we did a "simulation" to see what the potential distribution of steps in the organization might be once we rolled it out. The committee had what we thought was an ideal distribution based on Spotify's hiring strategy and what would make sense for an organization of our size. We asked each manager to estimate (in a non-binding way) which step each of their employees was on. We then combined these to get a master histogram of what the distribution might be. Luckily, we got a distribution reasonably close to what we were hoping for. So, it was a good validation of the Framework at that point. This also had the effect of making each manager have to apply the Framework in a concrete way, which also generated more good feedback.

I want to reinforce the issues we encountered by underestimating the efforts required from Compensation and Benefits and our back-office systems to support this work. While we involved HR from the onset, we didn't consider the timelines for the structural support to make the whole effort work. We should have involved those groups from the beginning, which would have avoided difficulties later.

CONCLUSIONS

I learned a tremendous amount in leading the effort around career pathing in the technology organization at Spotify. While I spent more time thinking about motivating and incentivizing employees than ever before, I also learned much more about my company and coworkers than I had expected. I was also reminded clearly how different my path had been from any of my fellow members of Technology. I had to put reasoning and explanation behind things I had learned experientially, which was incredibly valuable. Many of our employees had never previously worked at a company with career path support. Those with experience at other companies with career path frameworks had not seen anything similar to what the working group had created. As I talked with people individually and in small groups, I found better and better ways to articulate the reasoning behind the things that had just seemed obvious to us as we wrote the document. This process helped us immeasurably improve the document and hopefully helped clarify what I've written about in these chapters.

Creating this framework also raised some issues in the organization that we must address as a group. The Swedish word "lagom[62]" characterizes the culture of Spotify. We try to see each other always as equals. We encourage people to challenge their leaders if they don't think they are right. As the Steps document reflects, we put a higher value on strong teams than on strong individuals. We also imbue our teams and our individuals with autonomy in how they do their work. We tried to incorporate all of these ideas in our Career Steps. When people in the organization wish for more recognition and status to be reflected in our career pathing, is this counter to our culture, or is this indicative of the culture changing? What is the role of career pathing in enforcing a desired culture rather than supporting it? We'll continue to look at these questions as we evolve Career Steps.

Spotify is a unique company with a singular culture. The specifics of what we created and the lessons that we learned may or may not apply to your company. In aggregate, hopefully, you will find our experiences and learnings valuable as you think through how you want to do similar programs at your company.

CHAPTER 35

The Myth of the Startup in a Large Company

Originally published on August 10, 2014

I was reading a post from John Gruber[63], which had this paragraph in an ad for the iOS development team at Google:

My thanks to Google — that's right, Google (kind of awesome, right?) — for sponsoring this week's DF RSS feed. They're hiring developers and designers for their iOS app teams, which operate like a start-up within the walls of Google.

and I thought about the number of times I'd heard that line: "Operates like a startup within *<insert large company name here>*" or "Operates like a startup, but without the risk." I've heard that line many times from recruiters or friends. To be honest, I've even said it myself a few times, trying to sell a prospective candidate who I was trying to woo away from a startup.

That notion of working like you are in a startup but being part of a much larger organization is a myth. Anyone who says it is naive, disingenuous, or just plain wrong. Large companies that try to build those kinds of teams, be it "innovation lab," "startup experiment," or "corporate startup incubator," usually fail to achieve the innovation or energy they seek. The result is typically wasted money and angry employees who feel they were promised a bill of goods.

Stewart Butterfield, discussing the experience of selling Flickr to Yahoo said, "They sold out to Yahoo assuming that they'd be backstroking in rivers of money and terabytes of memory. Instead they had to fight for everything: servers, people, time.[64]"

Butterfield is talking about the inverse problem, but it comes down to the central crux of the issue at large companies: resource contention. It is a problem beyond the innovator's dilemma.[65]

In a startup, you spend all of your attention on finding the right product/market fit, finding customers, finding a flow of income, and/or finding investment. You will make the trade-offs you need to get your product off the ground. Often, this may mean choosing poor technologies in the short term to help you get going more quickly. Your resources are limited. You need to make do to get going. Maybe you will take some shortcuts in other areas just to get the product launched. You are fighting for your life and income and will do whatever it takes to get there. Why do you do it? Because you love the energy or are looking for the fiscal payoff. No risk, no reward.

In a big company, you don't have to make those trade-offs. There is probably a very mature infrastructure to build on, a brand to build off, and the promise of a paycheck, no matter the outcome. It is these conditions that destroy the innovation.

There is a mature infrastructure, but it may not fit what you are trying to build. Maybe you just need some minor tweaks, but the infrastructure team primarily focuses on serving the existing groups that bring in the revenue; it will be hard for them to prioritize your needs. Maybe you can even prototype or launch with your own skunkworks infrastructure; that won't last for long. The corporate infrastructure is vetted, financed, and regulatory compliant. They own their turf and don't appreciate someone jury-rigging something else.

There is a brand, but that brand is well-known and highly controlled. You can't launch just anything using that brand. It needs to be vetted. Instead of building your product, this means you focus on getting internal support. Maybe you launch under some new secret brand. This may work for a while, but if you are successful, there will be increasing pressure to join the fold. And in any case, launching under a secret brand kills the benefit of being part of the parent company.

The lack of risk is its own deterrent. Knowing that you get the paycheck is nice, but it is also understanding that you have little ownership of the outcome. It isn't "your" product. It is your corporation's product. You are just one of the people on the team. While you may still put in startup hours for the joy of it, eventually, you will realize that you aren't getting the startup reward for all your hard work, which is demoralizing.

The general problem is that even if you have the deep pockets of a large corporation backing you, you don't have the ability to do what it takes to survive. From the minute the project is launched, you are on a clock. You will be restricted from specific business models because you are part of a larger (presumably already profitable) parent. It's hard to justify spending a few years taking substantial losses to scale your business quickly when you are seen as a drain on the profits of your parent company. With its don't-ask-us-about-profits model, Amazon could never have been created as a division of Microsoft. The shareholders would have rebelled.

If you don't succeed quickly, the teams around you will covet your team's resources. They are like vultures waiting for you to fail, and they will rush to declare you a failure as early as possible if they think they can benefit from it.

If you are successful and start to grow, you have the same problem. Teams will attempt to co-opt your mission, take over your team, switch you onto the "official" technology stack, or flood you with resources trying to get some of your "startup" energy.

If you are successful by startup standards, that may not be seen as much of a success in a larger parent company with an established business. Being slightly profitable is a huge win for a startup; being barely profitable is a significant loss for an established corporation.

So, how can you create a startup in a large company? I think the university model is an interesting approach. Say you are Company X, a large multinational technology company, and you are constantly challenged by your inability to move at startup speed or innovate. Instead of creating a startup team inside some division, create an actual startup.

Solicit pitches from your entrepreneurial employees. Pick one or more, and fund them as independent companies. Give the founders an equity stake in the new venture, but your company will also own a significant stake, plus some non-exclusive licenses on the IP. Allow them to recruit from your company, but they will no longer be employees of your company. If the venture fails, they may be able to interview to rejoin their former company, and they may get some of their benefits back, but there is no guarantee of employment. Also, get them out of your building. Allow them to raise outside investment if they need it.

By sponsoring your employees, they are likely to build in a compatible way with your company's work, given that it is their training. They will know your industry. They won't be complacent because they can't afford to be. They will also be invested because they will directly benefit from their success. Ultimately, you will get the innovation you want, probably cheaper than if you tried to fund it within your cost structure with all of its overhead.

CHAPTER 36

Succession for Scale

Originally published on November 29, 2020

Recently, I have been thinking about how the role of the executive in a scaling startup evolves.

As a senior leader in a growing company, you need to be scaling faster than the organization. You grow by scaling yourself and the leaders in your team more quickly than the business. This fact is well known and is covered excellently in such books as **Zero to One** by Peter Theil and Blake Masters, and **The Hard Thing About Hard Things** by Ben Horowitz.

Even if you are aware of this fundamental requirement, it is still challenging to recognize when you are starting to fall behind on that scaling. The people on your team who got you to where you are today and who are working as hard as ever should be doing better than they are. You may start seeing the signs: teams falling behind, tensions between groups or functions, team leaders beginning to struggle with their work and increasing responsibilities.

You might not know what these scaling problems look like because you haven't seen them before. Maybe you do recognize them, but your loyalty to your team lets them go on longer than they should. You can get away with that for a while.

Eventually, your boss (the CEO, the board) or your peers start to recognize the growing gaps in your organization between where you are and where you should be. In a company with a good culture, they will let you know. In a company with a less open culture, your peers may notice but not feel like it is their place to say.

It will be nearly too late when the problems are apparent outside your team.

When these problems first arise, you need to put together a plan. You must act immediately if you missed the early signs and the challenges are visible outside your team.

You need to bring in new talent who can help close that gap. It will take time to do that. If you choose to re-double your efforts to mentor the existing folks, you will only fall further behind. Either you missed your mentorship window, your leaders need more mentorship than you can provide, or they are not yet ready to take on the new responsibilities in their role, even with mentorship.

Replacing people who have historically done well in their roles can seem cruel, which is why it is hard. It feels disloyal to the people who have been loyal to your company and helped build it with you. It is not their fault.

If you don't make those hard choices, though, they will be made for you by the person your boss or the board hires to replace you.

It doesn't have to be this way.

We have an assumption that in a growing company, people will remain in the roles they have had, and newer employees will come in below them. This assumption is one of the exciting incentives of joining a startup. It can be a career accelerator. Indeed, there are many stories of early startup employees remaining in their senior leadership roles through rapid growth and past the point of going public. Very few people are capable of this kind of speedy personal development, however.

Instead, we should be explicit about this challenge of growing a company. We should build a culture that acknowledges and celebrates this fundamental fact. Let people you hire know that you will support their growth, but be honest that if the company is scaling faster than they are, they may need to help hire the person who will help with the next phase in their role.

Reid Hoffman talks about these ideas in his book **_The Alliance_**. He discusses creating a "Tour of Duty," a compact of set length between the employer and employee that does not make expectations beyond that time.

I advocate for a more balanced and sustainable approach for companies that encourages employee development and business realities. Startups willing to hire at all experience levels and support employee growth can hire and retain better. Even those companies face challenges at their scaling inflection points when company leadership changes to the new business reality's necessities.

Suppose your company builds the concept of succession for scale into its culture. In that case, hiring your successor should be expressed as an opportunity for further mentorship and growth, not as a demotion or failure. Celebrate it as a rite of passage. Challenge the leaders in your team (and give them the tools) to recognize when this time has come and praise their self-awareness.

Build succession for scale into your compensation structure and leadership career pathing. Ensure that the newly hired leaders train the people they replaced to assume the role again in the future. When the position opens again, the person may now have the skills to step back into it.

Index

Footnotes

1. https://randsinrepose.com/
2. https://blog.kevingoldsmith.com/
3. https://en.wikipedia.org/wiki/Office_Assistant
4. https://youtu.be/NxcmoLKVd60?t=2m21s
5. https://en.wikipedia.org/wiki/The_Innovator%27s_Dilemma
6. https://engineering.atspotify.com/
7. http://theleanstartup.com/principles
8. https://blog.crisp.se/wp-content/uploads/2013/01/HowSpotify-BuildsProducts.pdf
9. https://steveblank.com/2013/07/22/an-mvp-is-not-a-cheaper-product-its-about-smart-learning/
10. https://thenewstack.io/the-rise-of-progressive-delivery-for-systems-resilience/
11. https://hbr.org/2016/02/a-refresher-on-statistical-significance
12. https://netflixtechblog.com/5-lessons-weve-learned-using-aws-1f2a28588e4c
13. https://netflix.github.io/chaosmonkey/
14. https://redmonk.com/jgovernor/2018/08/06/towards-progressive-delivery/
15. https://martinfowler.com/articles/feature-toggles.html
16. https://martinfowler.com/bliki/DarkLaunching.html
17. https://en.wikipedia.org/wiki/Blue-green_deployment
18. https://docs.gitlab.com/ee/user/project/canary_deployments.html
19. https://www.nytimes.com/2015/05/21/business/media/spotify-expands-to-include-video-and-predictive-playlists.html

20. https://en.wikipedia.org/wiki/Customer_lifetime_value

21. https://corporatefinanceinstitute.com/resources/management/management-by-objectives-mbo/

22. https://www.kevingoldsmith.com/talks/building-a-culture-of-continuous-improvement-in-your-company.html

23. https://www.kevingoldsmith.com/talks/organization-architecture-autonomy-and-accountability.html

24. *When I published this in 2014, this question frequently arose because two high-profile large companies in the industry were trying to change their cultures in very public ways: Yahoo and Microsoft.*

25. https://www.geekwire.com/2013/full-text-ballmer-memo-promises-one-strategy-microsoft/

26. http://allthingsd.com/20131108/because-marissa-said-so-yahoos-bristle-at-mayers-new-qpr-ranking-system-and-silent-layoffs/

27. https://www.itprotoday.com/cloud-computing/satya-nadella-memo-employees-about-layoffs

28. https://www.productplan.com/glossary/affinity-grouping/

29. https://en.wikipedia.org/wiki/Social-desirability_bias

30. https://theleanstartup.com/

31. https://sloanreview.mit.edu/article/toyotas-secret-the-a3-report/

32. https://www.product-frameworks.com/DIBB.html

33. https://www.youtube.com/watch?v=rwfXkSjFhzc

34. https://www.quora.com/What-qualities-should-a-software-engineer-have

35. https://www.omosola.com/

36. http://www.melconway.com/Home/Conways_Law.html

37. https://www.atlassian.com/agile/agile-at-scale/okr

38. https://en.wikipedia.org/wiki/Recency_bias

39. https://en.wikipedia.org/wiki/Recency_bias

40. https://www.idealrole.com/blog/affinity-bias.html

41. https://www.leadershipiq.com/blogs/leadershipiq/compliment-sandwich

42. https://en.wikipedia.org/wiki/Five_whys

43. https://en.wikipedia.org/wiki/Up_or_out

44. https://builtin.com/diversity-inclusion/unconscious-bias-examples

45. https://www.aihr.com/blog/9-box-grid/

46. https://www.youtube.com/watch?v=u6XAPnuFjJc

47. https://buffer.com/salaries

48. https://about.gitlab.com/handbook/total-rewards/compensation/compensation-calculator/

49. *thanks to Susanne Kaiser for the reference*

50. https://twitter.com/ReinH/status/1565487105907703808

51. https://www.greaterthancode.com/hosts/rein-henrichs

52. Toyota Production System https://global.toyota/en/company/vision-and-philosophy/production-system/

53. http://blog.crisp.se/2012/11/14/henrikkniberg/scaling-agile-at-spotify

54. To paraphrase, the system's speed is constrained to its' slowest part. (http://en.wikipedia.org/wiki/Amdahl's_law)

55. https://www.kevingoldsmith.com/talks/building-a-culture-of-continuous-improvement-in-your-company.html

56. https://en.wikipedia.org/wiki/Tuckman%27s_stages_of_group_development

57. Since the publication of this article, I have reconsidered my position after talking to multiple candidates who preferred pre-work assignments as a less stressful option. At Onfido and Anaconda, we gave our candidates multiple options for their technical assessment.

58. https://adadevelopersacademy.org/

59. https://apprenticareers.org/

60. Copy without understanding fully, see https://en.wikipedia.org/wiki/Cargo_cult

61. http://www.infoq.com/presentations/spotify-happiness-retention

62. https://en.wikipedia.org/wiki/Lagom

63. http://daringfireball.net/linked/2014/08/10/ios-at-google

64. http://www.wired.com/2014/08/the-most-fascinating-profile-youll-ever-read-about-a-guy-and-his-boring-startup

65. http://en.wikipedia.org/wiki/The_Innovator's_Dilemma

Acknowledgements

To my family who have supported me Nicole, and Lily Sophia. To my parents who inspired me.

I have learned so much from so many peers: Kevin Stewart, Maria Gutierrez, Meri Williams, Geoff Van Der Mere, Laurent Paris, Nicholas Harteau, Petter Wiederholm, Henrick Kniberg, Mikael Krantz, Marcus Frödin, Elise Shapiro, Viktor Cessan, Paul McKenna, Bob Jelica, Anders Ivarsson, and many others.

To the managers I've had who have been mentors and excellent examples to follow: Manny Vellon, Frits Habermann, John Metzger, Oskar Stål, Mark Britton.

Thanks to people who helped with editing the various chapters: Diane Guerts ("In 2018 Decide to Work Deliberately"), Ellie Spencer-Failes ("Taking a thoughtful approach to the job search process", "A resignation can be an opportunity", "Addressing the challenges of partially distributed engineering teams"), Hannah Davis ("The p-word"), Laura Blackwell ("Becoming a CTO", "The p-word", the "Writing Useful Performance Reviews" series), Mandy Mowers ("The p-word"), and Kate Stull ("The Spotify model: how to create, dissolve, and remix teams to be more dynamic and more innovative").

To the mentors and teachers who challenged and influenced me: Esther Derby, and Jerry Weinberg.

Kevin Goldsmith serves as the Chief Technology Officer for Distro-Kid, the world's largest digital music distributor. Previously, he was the CTO of Anaconda, Inc., the world's most popular data science platform with over 30 million users.

Before joining Anaconda, he served as CTO of AI-powered identity management company Onfido. Other roles have included CTO at Avvo, Vice President of Engineering, Consumer at Spotify, and nine years at Adobe Systems as a director of engineering. He spent eight years as a Lead and developer at Microsoft. He has also held software engineering roles at Silicon Graphics and IBM.

Goldsmith is the founder and principal at Nimble Autonomy, LLC., where he consults with growing startups working to scale their technology and teams deliberately and thoughtfully and with established companies working to be more innovative and agile in their product development practices.